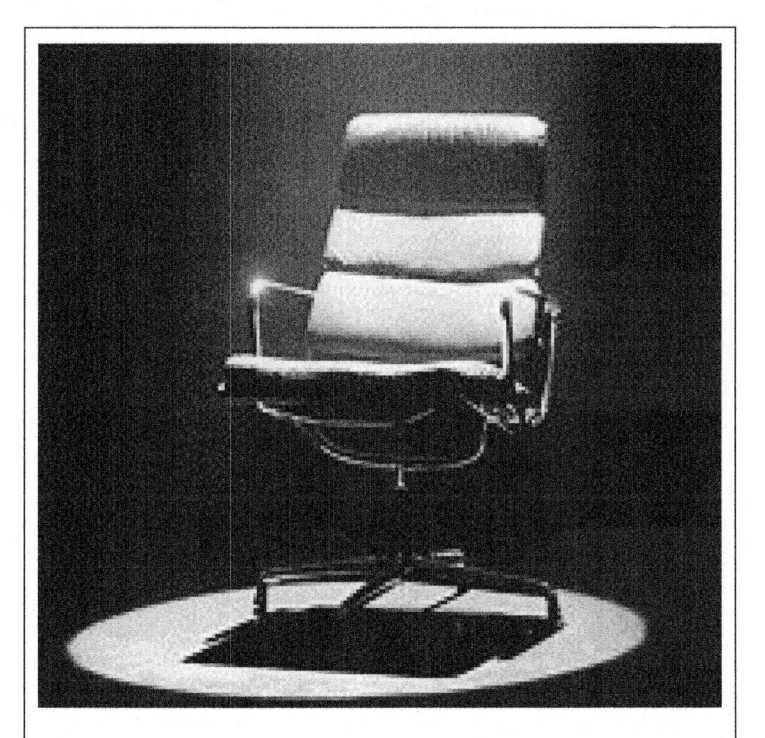

One general knowledge question had stumped every contestant since the programme began: "Why should any sane person play bowls?"

BOWLS
for the
BEWILDERED

Michael Coleman

ISBN 9798827470892

Text and Captions © Michael Coleman 2022

The right of Michael Coleman to be identified as the author of this work has been asserted by him in accordance with the Copyright, Design and Patents Act, 1988.

All rights reserved

email: bowls4bewildered@gmail.com

Independently published worldwide through Amazon KDP

Photo/Illustration Credits

Michael Coleman: viii, 26, 37, 42, 47, 97, 110, 117, 129, 131, 168, 193, 225; **Tom Pullin**: 81; **Sian Honnor/Bowls International**: 112; **Monte Fresco / Daily Mirror**: 57; **Old Book Illustrations**: 107, 118, 146, 171, 173, 178, 206, 211; **The Public Domain Review**: 34, 63, 125, 137, 143; **Pexels**: 38 (Oziel Gomez), 72 (Michael Burrows), 86 (Pew Nguyen), 87 (Saeed Khokar), 117 (Andres Ayrton), 134 (George Becker), 135 (Pixabay), 163 (Maitree Rimthong), 198 (Sonja Langford); **Picjumbo**: 104 (Viktor Hanacek); **Wikimedia Commons**: pp 15, 22, 28, 51, 53, 79, 92, 96, 101, 123, 144, 150, 153, 155, 160, 161, 166, 175, 180, 181, 184, 192, 201, 205, 213, 217, 220, 224, 288

Every effort has been made to confirm that the above photographs and illustrations, together with those not referenced, are either in the Public Domain or available for free use under a Creative Commons license. Assertions to the contrary should be directed to the above email address.

For members, past and present, of

Fareham Bowling Club
and
Palmerston Indoor Bowls Club

with thanks for sporting rivalry, companionship,
laughter and – ahem – inspiration …

About the Author

Michael Coleman is an award-winning children's author and educational scriptwriter.

His 70+ books have been translated into over 30 languages. Many are available in print and as e-books on Amazon or, if you don't mind library borrowers' graffiti, second-hand from 1p plus postage on Ebay. His radio and TV work for BBC Education has covered subjects as diverse as English, History, Drama, Religious Studies and a BAFTA-winning programme on Mathematics.

After damaging both knees playing football, and then leaving significant amounts of blood on cricket pitch and squash court, Michael finally took up bowls. In the years since, he has amassed a highly impressive catalogue of national, county and district titles that he's never come remotely close to winning.

This is his first book about bowls; and, once his clubs' disciplinary committees have clapped eyes on it, quite possibly his last.

After years of diligent research, the author had finally discovered the only sure-fire way of playing a dream game of bowls.

Author's Note

Bowls for the Bewildered is a (mostly) affectionate look at the unique sport of lawn bowls: truly a sport for all ages and physical abilities. As such, the book is sprinkled with chirpy references to the passing of years and the steady creep of infirmity. I make no apologies for this – and if you were my age, with my knees, neither would you.

I don't need telling, however, that I'm lucky. Many bowlers have embraced our game because of, or in spite of, physical conditions which did not creep up on them: conditions that they were either born with or had thrust upon them by life-changing events.

Nothing in what follows, therefore, should be taken as denigrating in any way bowlers with physical, sensory or learning disabilities (as supported by the coordinating charity *Disability Bowls England - DBE*) or those with visual impairment (as supported by their coordinating charity, *Visually Impaired Bowls England - VIBE*). Each and every one of them is an inspirational reminder of just what our sport is all about ... and why proceeds from this book will be donated to both DBE and VIBE.

These considerations aside, it's often said that much of bowls is played between the ears: that its highs and lows, joys and frustrations, are common to all. I really hope so: because then it should mean that every bowler reading this book is equally likely to find themselves muttering, "The cheeky sod! He's writing about me!"

Michael Coleman,
September 2022

bowls4bewildered@gmail.com
www.michael-coleman.co.uk

Contents

To Bowl, Or Not To Bowl 13
Drake's Pride 19
The Generations Game 25
Mission Impossible 31
Greens and Blues 41
The Name of the Game 49
Does My Bum Look Big In These? 55
Bowls for the Bewildered 61
Top (and Bottom) Gear 69
Playin' In The Rain 77
Chalk Talk 83
Line, Length and Condoms 89
Do Unto Others 93
Roll-Up, Roll-Up, Get Your Excuses Here! 99
Skips Ahoy! 105
Fours Play 111
Skip-Speak 121
Back To The Future 127
Offices of State 133
Looking In The Mirror 141
In Praise of Ham Salads 145
Your Very Good Health 151
Money, Money, Money 159
Booked Up 169

In League With Each Other	177
It's A Knock-Out	185
Marking Time	195
Birds Of A Feather	203
And The Winners Were	209
Keeping Your Head Down	215
The Final End	221

To Bowl, Or Not To Bowl

An admission. The title of this book is something of an abbreviation. The noble sport of bowls, or bowling, [1] produces brow-furrowing and head-scratching amongst many more souls than those who actually play the game. However, a title like *Bowls for the Doubtful, the Bewildered and the Utterly Mystified, Whether They Play the Game or Not* would have been pretty unwieldy – and extremely difficult to fit on the front cover.

Let us begin, then, by trying to identify the major inhabitants of what might be thought of as the 'bowls bewilderment spectrum'.

Shruggers

A typical Shrugger is somebody seeking a new outlet for their athletic and competitive energies who can't believe for one minute that bowls could be the answer. Not yet, anyway. Not while the majority of their body parts are still functioning adequately. Anyway, they shrug, what's the hurry? Surely a game as simple as this can be mastered in five minutes? Ten at the most. And will it even be worth the effort?

Frowners

Then we have those who, perhaps to prove a point to their bowls-mad neighbour, have taken the next step and tried the game – only to find that it doesn't seem to be quite as

---

[1] On no account should the reader confuse lawn bowls with the pastime of a similar name played on shiny wooden alleys and involving the attempted decapitation of ten 'pins'. Fortunately, the difference is easy to spot. If you find yourself having to insert your middle finger into an orifice then you're definitely not playing lawn bowls. If you find yourself playing with or against an anus, however, then there's a small chance that you might be.

simple as it looks. They frown. An illusion, surely. Give it a little time and they'll find the answer. They don't. Time goes on and before they know it they've passed the point of no return and become fully paid-up, card-carrying Frowners. Without treatment, tortured souls such as these can find themselves frowning their way up and down a section of the bewilderment spectrum which ranges from wondering if they'll live long enough to master the basic draw shot to wondering why on earth they ever took the bloody game up in the first place.

Smilers

Members of our third group are a complete mystery to a Frowner. These are the bowlers who give the impression of actually enjoying the game. They arrive with a spring in their step and – win, lose or draw – leave in the same cheerful manner. During a match they will frequently be seen to smile, laugh even. Naturally they celebrate their good shots, but also prove that they're human by cursing their bad shots as violently as any Frowner. The difference is that their essential *joie de vivre* soon resurfaces.

(These are generalisations, of course. They ignore the many possible variations in the same way that saying blue and green are colours of the rainbow ignores the multitude of bluey/greeny and greeny/bluey shades in between. Thus, if they've played a good enough shot, Frowners will occasionally smile. Likewise, given sufficient provocation – a melted chocolate biscuit at a game's midway break, for example – even the sunniest of Smilers may sometimes frown. More detailed studies of these endlessly fascinating types appear throughout the book. [2])

---

[2] In the interests of transparency, the author admits right now that he is a self-diagnosed Smiler-Frowner with gesticulatory complications. Nobody's perfect.

Shakers and Scoffers

Bowls bewilderment, however, is certainly not confined to those who play, or expect to play, the game. Arguably, it's even more pronounced in the category we must now brace ourselves to consider: the non-bowlers.

Arriving home from the bowls club, it was immediately apparent that their children had developed the DIY skills necessary to show how irked they were at their tea not being on the table again

Do not underestimate the size of this group. It is large and diverse. The non-bowling category encompasses those who are married to, or partnered with, or children of, or parents of, or otherwise related to, or friends with, or simply feel sorry for, somebody who plays bowls happily and contentedly. Individually, non-bowlers always need to be handled with care. If hunting in packs, they can only be handled with fire-proof gloves, if at all.

The bowler needs to be aware that there's a sliding scale for non-bowlers. At the tolerant end, are **Shakers**. Typically, they will react to their bowler's peculiar ways by shaking their heads and rolling their eyes. By-and-large they're supportive and understanding, working on the basis that a bowler indulged will - at some future date - be a bowler open to manipulation.

Scoffers, however, are way down at the other end of the scale; on bad days, off it completely. They make no bones about their view that bowls-playing is a complete waste of time, with bowls-players viewed in much the same light.

The difficulty for the bowler is that the same person can be both. An overlooked anniversary, a missed school play, or a couple of charred dinners may be all that is needed to turn the benevolent Shaker of the morning into the fuming evening Scoffer. Significant levels of bribery or grovelling may be needed to reverse the transition.

If there's a consolation for those faced with a Scoffer it's that they're following in a long and honourable tradition. Bowlers of yesteryear had to cope with them, too – and at a time when Scoffers had the power to do an awful lot more than make you spend a night in the spare room.

We are referring, of course, to the days when bowls' Scoffer-in-Chief was the monarch.

Beginning in 1363 with King Edward III, and continued by the equally misguided Richard II, Henry VII and Henry VIII, the game of 'bowles' - together with its far poorer relations football and 'gowfe' - was banned in favour of playing with bows and arrows.

To paranoid kings, worried about the ever-present threat of the country being invaded, the argument was that skill with the bow would be far more important to the common man should he ever be called upon to fulfil his involuntary duty as a member of the Middle Ages Home Guard. Anybody who has ever been struck on the shin by a fired bowl can see the flaw in this reasoning, but it probably made sense to the monarchs of the time.

To those who questioned the severity of the punishment for being caught playing bowls, Henry VIII would simply point out the very low numbers of second offenders.

Fortunately, by the time a serious invasion attempt *was* made, these dozy Kings had been replaced by a sensible Queen: Elizabeth I. She it was who had brought the game of bowls back in from the cold and allowed it to be played again.

This proved to be a decision of quite extraordinary prescience, for the attempted invasion would be repelled by none other than a player of bowls. A player, moreover, who still remains (much to the chagrin of the game's modern superstars) just about the most famous bowls player ever ...

Drake's Pride

That famous player was, of course, Sir Francis Drake - pirate, politician, rear-admiral and keen member of the Plymouth Swashbucklers Bowls Club – whose place in bowls lore was secured on 29 July 1588.
For the benefit of readers who may have forgotten much of the history they learned in school (or, in the case of younger readers, never studied at all) the background to the political situation at the time was as follows:
- Pope Sixtus V is the current head of the catholic Church of Rome which, more than 50 years after the event, is still seriously miffed about Henry VIII's creation of a breakaway protestant Church of England.
- The refusal of Henry's daughter, Elizabeth I, to yo-yo the country's religious allegiance back again is taking Sixtus' mifftedness up to a whole new level. He'd like to see England sorted out and Elizabeth replaced by one of his supporters.
- King Philip II of Spain fits the bill perfectly. He's a catholic, is jolly insulting about Elizabeth, and he really fancies adding 'King of England' to his CV.
- And so Philip gets together a fleet of fighting ships – *The Spanish Armada* – to do the business.

As we now know, his invasion plans came to a watery end. But, had they succeeded, the repercussions would surely still be echoing to this day. For example:
- o England would have reverted back to Catholicism: meaning that every Sunday morning the majority of the population would now not be setting foot inside an entirely different set of churches
- o The country's reputation for dodgy cooking would be even lower, due to its signature dish of paella and Yorkshire pudding

- Our football teams would have curious names like Real Macclesfield and Barnsleylona
- Retired criminals would have to travel a lot further afield, since running off to the Costa del Sol with their ill-gotten gains would be equivalent to trying to hide from the law on the Isle of Wight.

But, to repeat, Philip II's invasion attempt was a complete failure, with the much-vaunted Spanish Armada suffering an ignominious defeat.

We will have severe criticisms of our historians soon enough but for now they should at least be given credit for preserving the crucial fact that the hero of the hour was a bowls player.

When news came to Sir Francis Drake that the Armada had been spotted, we are reliably informed, our hero was on the bowling green. It is a measure of the man that his priorities were made clear at once, scoffing: [3]

> "Time enough to play the game
> and thrash the Spaniards afterwards"

It is at this point that our historians fail us completely.

Students eager to know the English and Spanish line-ups as battle commenced are given all the details. The weather conditions are described in full. A blow-by-blow account of the contest, complete with a full scorecard of ships engaged, sunk or hastily thrown into full-speed behind is readily available.

---

[3] Yes, Sir Francis Drake was clearly a bowls Scoffer. However, a clear distinction must be made. For a bowler to scoff at the puny challenge posed by their opponent is entirely different to a non-bowler's blasphemous scoffing at our noble game being played at all.

But nowhere can an answer be found to the question that would occur to any student of bowls: what was the result of the game that Drake insisted on finishing? It's as if the authors of the Gospels had all written down their different accounts of the Nativity but left out any mention of the baby Jesus.

Was Philip of Spain aware that his precious Armada was about to join battle with a fleet skipped by a bowler? We're not told, and yet only two possibilities exist: Philip either had no idea what he was up against, or else he was ridiculously over-confident.

Over-confidence is by far the most likely. Philip would have been a dyed-in-the-wool Scoffer, almost certainly having been brought up to regard the matador as a role model. Now bull-fighting no doubt requires a fair amount of bravery but (swords being longer than horns) it must also breed an over-reliance on superior weaponry. If this fails then a matador's Plan B can only be to run backwards as fast as possible.

Compare this with the bowler who stands on the mat needing to draw shot or go five down. Nerves of steel are required; veins coursing with iced water, not hot blood.

No, to any thinking bowls player there's only one way in which the Armada could have found itself facing an even contest: that is, if Drake had been a **Brooder**.

Put simply, Brooders are Frowners who don't leave their frowns behind. They take them home. More to be pitied than censured, a Brooder may replay events days – in the worst cases, weeks – after the game has finished.

This is why it's so astonishing that the result of Drake's bowls match hasn't been recorded.

How might the battle have panned out if he'd lost the match and been brooding angrily on the injustice of his opponent's lucky wick on the last end? Or if he'd been brooding miserably on the poop-deck about what minor flaw in his delivery action might be causing him to drop the occasional bowl short? Events would surely have turned out differently. But the records clearly show that neither applied. At all times during the battle, Drake was fully-focussed, thinking clearly and acting decisively.

He was, without any doubt, by far the worst Brooder in the club. Not only would he take his frowns home, he would leave his clothes behind.

It is down to we bowlers, therefore, to fill in the gaps left by the hopeless historians. Namely, that:

- Drake probably won his game.
- The likelihood is that he played well.
- And he was definitely not a Brooder.

In short, that King Philip II and his wretched Armada discovered to their cost what the record of history has so lamentably failed to pass down: that there are no more fearsome foes than bowlers at the top of their game.

In the heat of the battle, Sir Francis had completely forgotten Hint 101 from ye Bowles Englande Handbooke: "When aboard a fighting ship, never leave your bowles within reach of a gunner who may be running short of ammunition."

BOWLSPEAK

DRAW

The basic delivery in bowls, in which the player attempts the deceptively difficult task of getting their bowl to stop as close as possible to the jack.

Synonyms: lottery, lucky dip.

SHOT

The bowl which is currently closest to the jack.

Alternative definition: The bowl which is currently least furthest away from the jack.

HEAD

The developing cluster of bowls around the jack. As in life, the bigger the head the more objectionable.

Related phrases: headache, heading for trouble, head in the clouds and many more.

The Generations Game

The beauty of bowls is that it's a sport that can be played on level terms by those of any age, gender or physical capability. [4]

Shruggers will point to this statement as compelling evidence that the game must be too simple to bother about. Mentally they'll be comparing it to family pastimes such as Snakes and Ladders, Tiddlywinks or Dominoes. They are advised to read the opening sentence again. 'Sport' is a key word – meaning some sort of physical exertion. Even more important, though, is the phrase: 'level terms' – meaning that there are no bars to being either extremely good or absolutely hopeless at the game. No other sport can make this claim.

(The author is aware that darts has been proposed as a rival. Hmm. Certainly, young and old can be equally adept at burying a dart in the carpet – the young perhaps being more adept as they're closer to the ground.

And there is no disputing the beneficial effects that the game has on mental acuity. If an ability to count from 501 backwards is what's needed to get on in the world, then darts has no rival. Likewise, the game stands alone when it comes to factorising obscure numbers: {"sixty-seven to go out - she needs treble nine and double twenty, or seventeen and a bull's-eye, or a six, an outer bull and double eighteen, or ..."}.

But a 'sport' really does demand some form of physical effort and it is here that darts is found wanting. An activity in which the 'sporting' arm expends less energy

---

[4] For evidence, look no further than Nottinghamshire bowler Des Clark – at 87 years of age, as yet the oldest player to qualify for the National Bowls Championships Finals. In doing so, he had to beat off challenges from an 11 year-old and a 14 year-old.

than the other arm does in its lifting of the player's ever-present pint of best bitter surely fails the test. [5])

Back to bowls. The game's accessibility is both its biggest advantage and – in terms of its public perception – its greatest disadvantage. Strollers in the park see a couple of octogenarians playing bowls and automatically assume that it's a game for those on their last legs.

**Strength and energy fading, mental faculties on the wane – surely the day of reckoning couldn't be far off.
It was just a question of who would go first ... to join the bowls club.**

---

[5] Some critics are less tolerant, going so far as to assert that the only way in which the words 'darts' and 'sport' can ever legitimately appear in close proximity to each other is in a sentence like: '"Thanks, Sport!" laughs the Australian pickpocket as he darts away with my wallet.'

Bowls clubs themselves can unwittingly reinforce this view. Accepting sponsorship from the developers of retirement villages and care homes doesn't help. Neither do boards around the green advertising funeral plans or the services of solicitors offering help on all aspects of will-writing. Links with firms of financial advisers adept at the avoidance of inheritance tax compound matters.

Is it any wonder that the world is full of Shruggers who not only think that bowls is a simple game but one that they – not yet having one foot in the grave – are simply too young to start playing?

Nothing could be further from the truth, as a quick look at the make-up of the gold medal-winning women's triple at the 2022 Commonwealth Games reveals:

- Jamie-Lea Marshall (b.1990) started playing bowls at the age of 10
- Natalie Chestney (b.1989) couldn't wait that long and began aged 9
- Sian Honnor (b.1988) started almost before she'd learned how to count the candles on her birthday cake – at the tender age of 7

Do the math, as our transatlantic friends say. All three are in their early thirties and have been internationals since their twenties or before.

This will make uncomfortable reading for Shruggers, young and old. (If bowls is a game for all ages, so too is shrugging).

To the pre-pubescent Shrugger the message is clear: if you want to be a bowls champion with legions of adoring social media followers then the time to put your phone down and get off the sofa is NOW!

As for older Shruggers – and even more so for their arrogant relations the super-Shruggers (those who not only regard the game as trivial but also firmly believe that having quickly mastered it post-retirement their international call-up will soon follow) the message is stark: you'll be 50 years too late, Sunshine!

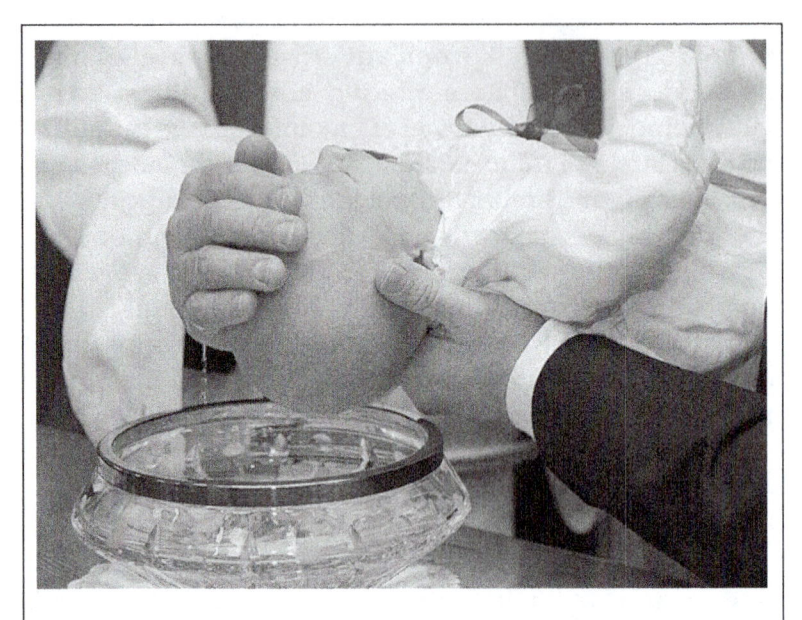

Having had their preferred boys' names of Lignoid, Henselite and Grippo all vetoed by the vicar, the bowls-mad couple reluctantly settled for Jack.

A vibrant bowls club, then, will be rather like a multi-generational family. There will be noisy, energetic youngsters. Middle-aged parents will rub shoulders with older-aged grandparents, some of them acting soberly and others doing their level best to out-junior the juniors. And there will be the elder statesmen and stateswomen, still able to bowl a decent bowl in between telling anybody who will listen about how it wasn't like this when I was your age.

As with any family, tensions are inevitable. Older members will occasionally bridle at the screeching of an enthusiastic junior, especially when they become aware of it whilst driving to the club, windows up, hearing aids off and still two streets away. And the enthusiasm of even the most effervescent youngsters could be dampened by continually having to wait on the mat whilst their playing partners get their breath back after changing ends.

Ultimately, though, what divides bowlers is far less than what unites them: the shared desire to get to grips with an impossible game ...

The junior members were always complimentary about the seniors' playing standards, but their body language told an entirely different story.

BOWLSPEAK

TRAILING THE JACK

Moving the jack from where it was to where it wasn't. This is a good thing if where it was wasn't good and where it wasn't was, but bad if where it wasn't wasn't bad and where it wasn't wasn't anything like as good.

Related phrases:

(*bad movement*) Jack it in!

(*good* movement) I'm all right Jack.

KITTY

Colloquial name for the jack, the feline provenance of which is obscure. It's possibly linked to the fact that a shot which ends up trailing the jack / kitty is bound to leave somebody feeling decidedly pussed-off

Mission Impossible

In the short story *The Heel Of Achilles*, by P.G. Wodehouse, a brusque, go-getting businessman decides to take up golf in order the win the heart of the girl he loves. When he's about to have the game explained to him at length by an afficionado, he interrupts what promises to be a lengthy discourse with the demand, "Keep the reminiscences ... tell me in as few words as you can just what it's all about."

And the answer he receives is: "You hit a ball with a stick until it falls into a hole."

The aim of most sports can be compressed in a similar way. For example:

- *Football* is about kicking or heading a round ball into a goal
- *Rugby* involves carrying an oval ball over a line, ideally without leaving any limbs behind
- *Badminton* is about hitting a bunch of feathers over a net so that they don't come back again
- *Cricket* is ... the exception that proves the rule

So, for the benefit of those bewildered about the aim of bowls, the simple Wodehousian explanation would be that a player endeavours to ...

Propel a round object (a "bowl" or "wood") across a smooth, flat surface (a "green") so as to finish as close as possible to a target ball (a "jack") [6]

---

[6] We do not intend to burden the reader with more details about the game than necessary. After all, the current (4th) edition of *Laws of the Sport of Bowls* runs to some 63 pages, comprising 5 major sections, 18 sub-sections, loads of sub-sub-sections and – as if that isn't enough – 3 appendices. Hopefully, our ignoring much of what's contained in this document should not present a problem; most bowlers manage to do so for the whole of their careers.

Nobody really knew what cricketers did, but there was common agreement that they looked awfully silly while they were doing it.

Reading this simple explanation, who could blame a Shrugger for shrugging or a Scoffer for scoffing until they choked? However, if each of the key items is examined more closely an altogether different picture emerges ...

"JACK"

What isn't mentioned in the definition is that the jack has to be at least 23 metres away from the bowler. However, it's allowed to be as far off as 36 metres – a distance which invariably has the club wag calling for opera glasses or the club telescope.

The other unmentioned problem is that although the jack must begin in a central position there's no guarantee that it will stay there. The thing can quite legitimately be moved, either deliberately or accidentally.

This happens so regularly that if sports items were capable of developing a persecution complex, bowls jacks would be queuing for therapy along with cricket balls and shuttlecocks.

"BOWL" (or "WOOD")

Two names are used for this central item in the game simply because bowls were once made of (very hard) wood. Nowadays they're made from composite stuff, but – especially amongst bowlers with long memories – the alternative name still lingers. [7].

A more detailed discussion of the pros and cons of different bowls appears later. For now it is simply sufficient to point out the one thing that all bowls have in common: they do not run in a straight line. They are designed to travel along a curved path, some curvier than others.

In short, bowls are the sporting equivalents of news media: they are biased. They can swing to the left or they can swing to the right, but the one thing you can't expect from them is that they're going to be straight with you.

Why this should be so, and who to blame for it, are facts that have been lost in the mists of time but there's historical evidence that bowls have been biased since 1560 at least. Originally achieved by the use of weights, the bias is now determined by the shaping of the bowl.

---

[7] For the terminal Frowner this modern development means that a set of bowls which obviously aren't doing what they're told can no longer be tossed onto a bonfire. Composites will simply rise, like charred but tormenting phoenixes, from the ashes. True 'woods' burn beautifully and for long enough to ensure that the things are left in no doubt about who was boss in the end.

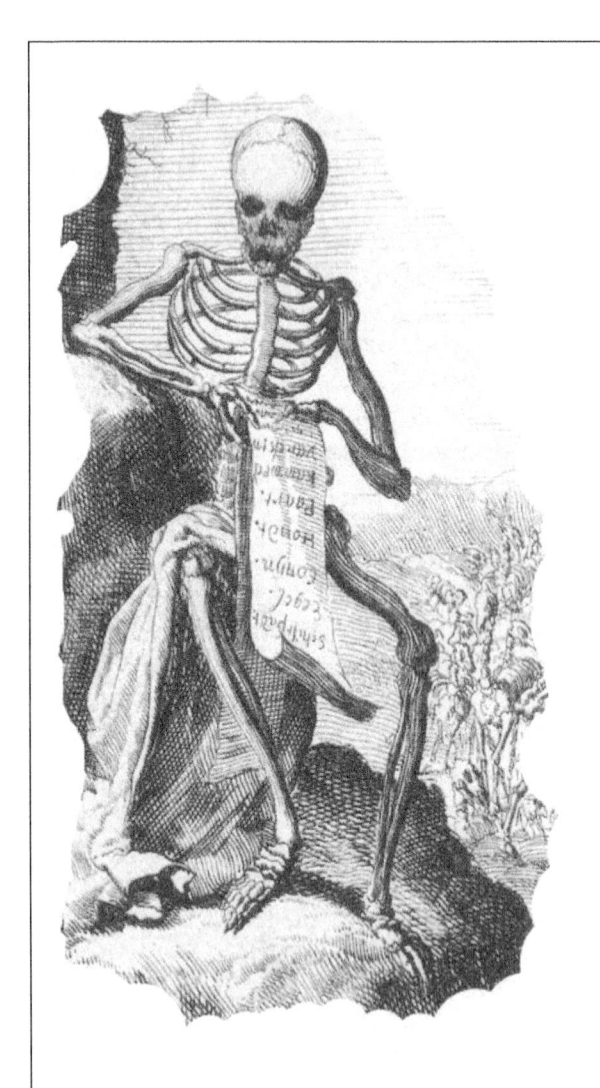

"In fiery pit 21345276141267:
Genghis Khan, Lucrezia Borgia,
Vlad the Impaler ...
and the inventor of biased bowls."

Whether this bias is relatively slight or seriously profound, the basic principle is unchanged: aim your bowl at the jack and the thing will curve away from it. It's a counter-intuitive lesson that comes as a revelation to a Shrugger: you cannot aim at the target you're trying to hit. [8]

"GREEN"

The definition describes the "green" – that is, the playing surface – as 'smooth' and 'flat'. These two adjectives could keep officers of a trades descriptions department busy for the rest of their working careers.

Let us be clear and unequivocal. No green is completely smooth. Nor flat. It may – and, compared to the bowler's scruffy patch of lawn, will - *look* smooth and flat. When walked upon, it may *feel* smooth and flat. But the reality is that this smoothness and flatness is an optical illusion – or, more accurately from the gullible and trusting bowler's point of view, an optical delusion.

Examine any green closely (and it doesn't always have to be that closely). It will be discovered to have little bumps, ridges and hollows. The grass will be longer in some places and shorter in others. Parts will be lush, and others – perhaps where the watering system hasn't reached or a member's dog has, strictly against club regulations, relieved itself – may be bare.

Any of these imperfections can throw a bowl off its intended course and lead it to finish even further away from the jack than it might have done. (Conversely, they

---

[8] The significance of this should not be underestimated. Imagine that bullets were bowls. Would lawmen like Wyatt Earp have been so effective if, in order to plug the baddie leaning against the saloon bar, they'd been unable to aim between his eyes but been forced to take a line on the fifth whisky bottle to the right (or left, if shooting backhand)? The whole history of the Wild West might have been altered.

could divert a badly-directed bowl into something far better – a topic considered elsewhere).

Add this lot together and it can be seen that our simple definition, in the interests of accuracy and honesty, needs to be extended.

Thus: in bowls, a player endeavours to -

> **Propel a round object (a "bowl" or "wood")**
> **<u>which does not run in a straight line and often seems to have a mind of its own</u>**
>
> **across a smooth, flat surface (a "green")**
> **<u>which may look smooth and flat but is nothing like it, whatever the greenkeeper says</u>**
>
> **so as to finish as close as possible to**
> **a target ball (a "jack")**
> **<u>which could be absolutely anywhere except where it was always placed when the player was learning the game</u>**

The author offers this definition, copyright-free, to the authorities for use in any promotional literature they may care to develop. It has much to commend it.

For a start, it's a definition that's guaranteed to make the average Shrugger think a little more deeply about the game they're treating so dismissively.

Far more importantly, it may play a small part in the worthy cause of helping Frowners to become Smilers. Study the expanded definition closely, and the average Frowner may begin to see the futility in frowning because their bowl hasn't finished closer to the jack. They will see the impossibility of what they've tried to do and accept what the Smiler knows intuitively: that it's nothing short of a miracle that their bowl has got a close as it has.

The green looked flat but he was not a bowler who left things to chance.

Footnote: Mission Really Impossible

Notwithstanding the section just ended, this book is about lawn bowls as played on what is generally accepted to be a 'flat' green. However, it is has to be pointed out at this stage that a mutation exists called 'crown green' bowls.

This version of the game cleverly avoids any criticism of the flatness of the green by being played on a surface deliberately contrived to be anything but.

A typical crown green will rise from its perimeter to a sort of burial mound in the centre, but it could equally well be undulating, giving the distinct impression of having been designed by the same malign imagination as a putting green at St. Andrews. [9]

It was certainly one of the trickier crown greens but the view from the top was worth it

Crown green bowls differs from its flat green cousin in other ways, the most notable of which are:

---

[9] The author wishes to state here and now that he does not share the intolerant view of some flat green bowlers that crown green is 'a game for pillocks played on hillocks'. The same goes for the view of the odd crown greener that flat green bowls is 'a game on the flat played by a twat'.

- Not only are the bowls biased (of course) but so is the jack
- Games are not confined to travelling up and down narrow strips (rinks) of the green, but can head off in any direction

These are the bare bones. Open-minded readers who want to learn more about crown green bowls are advised to pay a visit to their local library. [10]

Searching the books catalogue for the topic, 'bowls: crown green' is the obvious first step.

If that draws a blank, try 'masochism: advanced.'

---

[10] Readers should be aware that since they last paid it a visit, their library may well have been re-branded as a 'discovery centre'. The adjective is there as a warning. What with having to negotiate the new café area, soft play area, comfortable chairs, magazine racks and ranks of computer terminals, it may take some time to discover where the books live.

BOWLSPEAK

MAT

The oblong thing you must have one foot either on, or above, when you deliver your bowl.

FOREHAND

As viewed from the mat, the right-hand side of the rink for a right-handed player, the left-hand side for a left-handed player. This also applies when you get to the other end, even though left is now right and right would be wrong.

BACKHAND

See 'FOREHAND' and stand on your head.

HAND

Confusingly, a word which can refer either to the forehand or the backhand. If a player isn't doing too well on one side of the rink, it might be suggested that they 'try the other hand'. This means playing the backhand if they've been using the forehand or having a go on the forehand if they've been playing the backhand. On the other hand, if they've been using the other hand then it'll be the other hand.

The simplest thing is to remember that 'HAND' as used in bowls is a kind of shorthand.

Greens and Blues

What is claimed to be the world's oldest existing bowling green can be found in Southampton, on the south coast of England. Known, accurately if rather unimaginatively, as *Southampton (Old) Bowling Green*, its history can be reliably traced back to 1299.

A second date of interest, not only to bowlers but also to players of the many other (albeit inferior) sports which require a large area of cultivated grass, is that of 31st August 1830. It was on this day that an unsung hero named Edwin Beard Budding patented his invention: the lawnmower. Hand-pushed, with a width of just 480 mm (19 inches), it doesn't compare to today's motorised, precision versions, naturally. But in 1830 it was a quantum leap from what had gone before.

Until then, the choice faced by a bowling club needing to keep the grass below head height was either:
    a)   quickly and efficiently-operated scythes, or
    b)   rather slower domesticated grazing animals – typically, sheep or goats

The disadvantages of each are pretty obvious. Scythe operators have working days and need to be paid, yet even the most skilled will leave behind a stubble of sorts.

By comparison, sheep and goats are perfectly happy to work far longer hours, for well below minimum wage and, given enough time, can produce an almost stubble-free playing surface. Unfortunately, these woolly lawn-mowers inevitably leave behind an entirely different residue which has to be cleared before play can begin.

But the gratitude owed by lawn bowlers to Edwin Budding's invention and its descendants is but part of the story. It takes more to maintain a bowling green than a Sunday morning whack over with a Flymo. For all the earlier talk about the non-smoothness and non-flatness of

Novice: "How can you tell the bowls from the turds?"
Expert: "The bowls flatten your rhubarb."

any bowling green, compared to the average lawn they are as smooth and flat as an oil-slicked billiard table. Achieving this state is the responsibility of yet another unsung hero/heroine: the greenkeeper.

Greenkeepers tend to be shadowy figures, doing their work unseen. In a way, they're a bit like knees and bladders: taken for granted until they're not doing their job properly. And doing that job properly involves rather more than knowing how to start the mower and in which direction to point it.

The black arts of greenkeeping are beyond the scope of this book. Suffice it to say that 'bewildering' is an apt description of just how much a greenkeeper has to know.

Think of them as GP's for grass. [11] They need to be aware of health-promoting measures such as scarification and top-dressing, of course. But being able to spot and treat such nasty lurgies as dollar spot and take all patch, and even be able to pronounce the likes of anthracnose and microdochium (fusarium) patch, takes all the knowledge and skill of a seasoned practitioner.

In short: if your bowl doesn't end up where intended – even though, of course, you did everything perfectly – you can blame the bowl; you can blame the green; but only the foolhardy will blame the greenkeeper.

The greenkeeper – fondly referred to as GK by all at the club – had finished work. He'd brushed, swept and double-mowed the glistening turf. With final whispered words of endearment GK turned his back on the green, stored his equipment in the greenkeeper's shed, then hurried away.

He'd just reached the club's front gate when Madam President puffed up behind him. "GK," she trilled. "Wait a moment. Can I ask you a question? It's been on my mind for some time."

"Ar," nodded the greenkeeper reluctantly.

"You do such a wonderful job with our green," said Madam President, "but then you always disappear without waiting to see how it plays. I've always wondered why."

GK sucked his teeth, rubbed his stubbly chin, then surprised Madam President by pointing out towards the club car park.

"That be your car, Ma'am?" he asked.

Madam President's eyes moistened and her voice dropped to an emotional purr. "It is," she said, looking

---

[11] Except that it's easier to get an appointment to see a greenkeeper.

fondly at the glistening car in the President's allocated parking spot. "My pride and joy,"
"Care for it regular, eh Ma'am?" asked GK.
"Oh, yes! Every week, without fail. It's washed and polished and waxed and buffed until I can see my face in it."
GK sniffed. "And how you'm feeling when some pigeon comes along and craps all over it?"
Madam President's ice-blue eyes narrowed alarmingly. "Murderous!" she spat in fury. "It happened only last week. If I could have got my hands on the thing I'd have wrung it's bloody neck!"
From the clubhouse changing rooms came the raucous sounds of club members pouring out onto the green, soon followed by the clack of bowls and jolly cries of "wrong bias!"
Shielding his eyes, the greenkeeper hurried off, calling over his shoulder as he went, "Right. Now you'm know why I disappear!"

Nowadays grass is not the only playing surface used to bewilder bowlers. The game is increasingly being played on what are advertised by their manufacturers as durable, resilient, multi-functional outdoor and indoor surfaces – the accepted technical shorthand for which is 'carpet'.

As their supporters will point out, bowls carpets have a host of advantages over grass:

- ✓ Carpets aren't alive, so don't need feeding and watering
- ✓ They don't attract nasty diseases which cause them to fade, wilt or die

- ✓ Carpets don't grow, so don't have to be mown every five minutes
- ✓ Given the above – expensive greenkeepers are no longer needed. A carpet can be vacuum cleaned by any member happy to wear a pinnie
- ✓ Unlike grass, which limits play to the 'summer' – that is, the theoretically drier and warmer period between early April and late September [12] – a carpet can be played on all the year round. As a drier alternative to a dip in the ocean, dedicated bowlers can even don hats, scarves and thermal underwear for a game on Boxing Day
- ✓ Twelve-months-a-year bowling means twelve-months-a-year income for the club
- ✓ Construct a building round the carpet, add a well-stocked bar and dining room and you've got a wind- and rain-free place that can be marketed as an Indoor Bowling Club

Against points such as these, detractors will make the following arguments about bowls carpets:

- ✗ They don't play like grass
- ✗ They don't feel like grass
- ✗ They don't smell like grass
- ✗ They don't look like grass
- ✗ In short, they're not grass

Whether or not bowls will increasingly be played on carpets rather than grass remains to be seen. If the noble art of greenkeeping goes the same way as thatching a

---

[12] In the UK; bowlers in other parts of the world should adjust the months as necessary.

roof then the chances are that carpets will gradually become as common as tiles.

However, although games on a carpet certainly feel different to those on grass, the emotions remain the same.

A Frowner on grass will be a Frowner on a carpet, only with drier feet. Smilers on grass will become even bigger Smilers if, when playing on a carpet that could double as an oil slick, they not only manage to keep their bowls in the same town but also on the same rink as the jack.

In the winter many bowlers already switch from grass to carpet quite happily. It could just be that it will become easier than many think to accept surfaces which don't feel, smell or play like grass.

Not looking like grass could be a lot trickier, though. A nasty precedent has been set. The finals of the World Bowls Tour Indoor Championships are played on a carpet that is not green, but *blue*. Is this a step too far?

For example, when exhorting their team-mates not to underestimate the curve their bowls need to arrive at the jack, players the world over have become used to crying, "take enough green!" Can they become used to yelling, "take the blue!"?

Or even, at the most mundane level, reporting to their nearest and dearest that they're off to the bowling blue for an hour?

It doesn't sound right - yet. Perhaps it just needs time. After all, other references have been assimilated without difficulty. Frowners and – even more so – Brooders will admit to 'feeling blue' after a bad game.

And 'turning the air blue' has surely got a pedigree as long as the game itself.

The President's shrewd bargaining at the market stall next to his Moroccan holiday villa may indeed have saved the club a small fortune, but members still had the uneasy feeling that the new carpet wasn't what they'd voted for at the AGM.

BOWLSPEAK

WRONG BIAS

A bowl released the wrong way round, so that it curves away from the jack rather than towards it. Usually greeted by derisive cat-calls and finger-pointing.

Ironically, players achieving much the same result – even though the bowl was delivered the right way round – are treated with far more sympathy.

Related phrases: Is the bar open?

WICK

A deflection, resulting in a badly-directed bowl finishing in a favourable position.

Synonyms: Local knowledge

Related phrases: (sarcastic) wick-ed; (non-sarcastic) this is getting on my bloody wick

The Name of the Game

English is a wonderful language.

It's perfectly true that, when spoken, English has its limitations. It doesn't have the mellifluous and romantic cadences of French, for example. In the winter months, nothing can beat the phlegm-loosening and throat-clearing benefits of barking German. And for bowlers prone to displays of histrionics, Italian will always be the language of choice. [13] When it comes to a language in which to express shades of meaning, though, English simply cannot be beaten. English, to use a French word, has *nuance*.

(That's right, English – a language with more shades of meaning than you can shake a stick at – doesn't have a word for 'shades of meaning'. It has had to borrow one from French, a language with limited shades of meaning but which nevertheless does have a word for 'shades of meaning'. No wonder the English and the French don't get on.)

Consider as an example, the typical pairs match. For the benefit of any Scoffer who may have picked up this book whilst their bowler has gone AWOL, ready to throw at them on their return, pairs teams in bowls comprise a lead and a skip. The leads deliver their bowls whilst the skips stand up at the other end of the rink directing

---

[13] For proof, if proof is needed, one need look no further than the Italian phrase *Prima Donna*. Literally 'first lady' it's a term universally accepted as describing anybody who is behaving in a temperamental fashion and/or has an over-inflated view of themselves. In the unlikely event that UK readers can think of a member of their bowls club to whom this description could be applied, they're urged to show understanding, Remember that Britain was occupied by the Romans for the best part of 400 years; even after all this time, some of the genomes responsible could still be doing the rounds..

operations. Once this is done, the skips and leads change places and the skips deliver their bowls. Now, ignore the bowling part and consider solely the bit in the middle: the changeover.

The simple way of describing what happens is to say that both players *walk* from one end of the rink to the other. The glories of nuance, however, give so much more descriptive scope.

If the game has nothing at stake the players could be said to:
- stroll
- amble
- meander

Should the two leads be on unusually friendly terms, they might even link arms and:
- promenade
- cake-walk

If one of the leads has played a particularly good shot or two, however, they will find it almost irresistible to
- swagger
- strut

On the other hand, leads who have either dropped their bowls woefully short or buried them in the ditch will undoubtedly:
- skulk
- slink

Most of these variants apply to skips as well, of course, but there are some that are particularly relevant to them:
- saunter (*supremely confident*)
- stride (*at last, my turn*)
- stalk (*watch, Oh lead of mine, and learn!*)

He would spend many a holiday hour practising his "guess who's got a toucher!" changeover gambol – in the fervent hope that one day he'd actually get to use it.

(One possibility that should not be included is *skip*. A skip should never skip. It lacks the necessary *gravitas* that the role demands)

Finally, if the match is taking place after the club bar has been open for a good while, we might add to the list:
- totter
- stagger
- roll

Hopefully, the point has been made. If you want a word for something, the chances are that English has choice aplenty.

So what happens when we consider the name of our game: bowls? Here, it's a noun. But the same word, *bowls*, is also a verb; it's used to describe what a bowler does.

> ***"Bowl: To roll (a ball, hoop etc) smoothly along the ground"***
>
> *Chambers Dictionary*

Now let's apply the nuance test to find a few shades of meaning for this humble word.

The author put his online thesaurus to the test. It came up with a list of possibilities that were so hopeless he's still mulling over whether or not to demand a refund – namely:

- Throw
- Chuck
- Lob
- Hurl
- Fling

Now it's certainly true that each of these words is often an accurate description of deliveries that will be seen on any bowling green. But by no stretch of the imagination can they be considered to satisfy the vital element of the bowl travelling '*smoothly* along the ground'. A bowl that is chucked or hurled or even flung may well result in a bowl that finishes close to the jack, but *bowled* it has not been.

The purist will argue that this lack of possible words to describe what a bowler does means that there's only one acceptable way of doing it: to bowl.

Those on the other side will argue that an octogenarian with a bad back hasn't got much choice in the matter – they have to shoot from the hip because they can't get any lower.

Greenkeepers will argue back that if their chucking is going to bugger up their lovely green then they shouldn't be playing bowls at all; they should be under the trees on a Parisian side street, lobbing boules and slaughtering unwary pigeons.

In hindsight, the Membership Secretary saw that she should really have enquired of his previous club as to how "Bomber" Briggs got his nickname

This is a debate that's probably as old as the game itself. Sir Francis Drake may have been a Chucker, we don't know. (Yet another black mark for the historians).

So, let's end by raising some questions for post-match discussion over a friendly drink:
- How important is Newton's Third Law of Motion? (Which, as savvy bowlers won't need reminding, states that for every action there's an equal and

opposite reaction). This suggests that when a bowl lands on the green at an angle, the green pushes back and reduces the bowl's speed. [14] Thus, those who bowl will have to put in less effort than those who chuck. Does this mean that those who chuck because they've got bad backs will end up with even worse backs and have to chuck even harder and end up with ...?

- What do the star bowlers on the telly do? Is it true that those who *don't* deliver their bowls smoothly can be counted on the fingers of one amputated finger?
- Will the bowling/chucking debate even matter if grass is gradually phased out in favour of carpet – especially if the carpet is laid on a sub-base of reinforced concrete?

---

[14] For verification, drop it vertically – preferably not on your foot – and see how far it rolls forward.

Does My Bum Look Big In These?

A riddle.
- Top golfers use them
- Top tennis players swear by them
- Top footballers swear by them and at them [15]
- Top track and field athletes all depend on them
- The Shrugger who finally decides to have a crack at bowls will be initiated by them but, after a few sessions, will join the rest of the club's members and have nothing more to do with them

What are they?

Answer: Coaches

It's a paradox, really. Every bowls club has its coaching team. They are often the first members that prospective bowlers encounter. If they don't do their job well, they're also the last members these prospective bowlers see as they march out of the gates to become life-time Scoffers. Why aren't the coaches always as revered as they should be?

Latent snobbery, perhaps. Club champions are often too busy becoming club champions to become qualified coaches. The same goes for the trying-to-become-club-champions. The result is that the coaching team are not always the best bowlers in the club. So ... what gives them the right to teach others the finer points of a game they haven't mastered themselves?

---

[15] Footballers swear at everybody, of course, especially the match officials. But, to give them their due, lip-read a televised match and you'll see that they're generally even-handed. For every suggestion that the officials were born out of wedlock there'll be another which compliments them on still being sexually active.

The bewilderment of those who think this way is easily explained: they are confusing an ability to play the game well with an ability to teach others how to play the game well.

For example, having seen his fellows sporting the latest in bowls shorts, a man tries a pair on and inevitably wonders: does my bum look big in these?

Will he only accept an answer from a haute couture bowls shorts designer? Or from a Harley Street cosmetic surgeon with a buttock specialism? Of course not. He will seek the judgement of his beloved, a person who has an eye for what he looks good in and who – presumably – is familiar with the bum under consideration. And he will accept her answer, whether it be "No", "Fairly" or "Of course it does! Your bum would look big in a bell-tent. You've got a big bum, dearest. Get over it. Be grateful you've found something you can squeeze it in to. Let's go!"

Club coaches, then, have a perfect right to be club coaches. So what lessons will they endeavour to pass on to their usual clients, the new bowlers?

The mechanics of grip, of how best to hold the bowl, is likely to be an early topic. Beginners are likely to hear about the pros and cons of claw grips, cradle grips and their variations. Finger and thumb positions will be covered to reduce the chances of the bowler being all fingers and thumbs.

Delivery styles – the crouch delivery, the semi-crouch delivery, the arm delivery with one leg stuck out and an improbable angle – will follow.

After this, there'll be advice on combining grip and delivery style so as to send the bowl on its way. Hopefully it's at this point that coaches will impress upon their charges the importance of the bowl being released smoothly, and that what worked for Barnes Wallis against

Vincent's reverse claw grip was unorthodox, but surprisingly effective.

the Möhne dam in WWII is not conducive to the consistent results they're after.

In the sessions that follow, exercises involving paper squares, jacks at different lengths and the mat in different places will be supplemented by little practice games designed to reinforce these basic lessons.

It is at this point that the student is likely to cast a casual eye at the bowlers on the non-coaching rinks and - seeing as many grips and delivery styles as bowlers - innocently ask why. And the good coach will reluctantly admit that theory and practice can sometimes part company – and that the ultimate test of the game is not how the bowl is delivered but where it ends up.

This naturally prompts the obvious follow-up question (usually unvoiced, unless the student is a Scoffer acting under cover), which is: why have I had to go through your hours of diligent instruction?

Well ... it's said that the lessons a student really learns at university are those that remain after they've forgotten everything they've been taught: namely, essential life skills such as sociability, independence of thought and how to down a pint in under ten seconds.

So it is with bowls club coaching. The best coaches don't just show their pupils how to play the game; they also, far more importantly, show them how the game is to be played.

They are, almost without exception, Smilers. They are instinctively optimistic, believing that with practice even the most hopeless duffer can improve – and, even if they don't, an enthusiasm for the game is what matters most. [16] Enthusiasm: whether they do it consciously or not, this is the bowls life-skill that good coaches impart. If their enthusiasm for, and love of, the game could be bottled then the profits of the average club bar would increase overnight. [17].

Sadly it's a life skill that often gets submerged under the waves of competitive play, surfacing only during the occasional roll-up game before diving to the sea-bed

---

[16] To be true, coaches can sometimes be *too* optimistic. Rarely, if ever, will they suggest to an utterly hopeless beginner that their time might be better spent doing something – anything – other than playing bowls. But with the siren voice of the club treasurer murmuring in their heads, "membership fee, membership fee," even this failing can be excused.

[17] These are people, remember, who spend hours and hours at their bowls clubs *not playing bowls!* Shakers and Scoffers are invited to get their heads round that one.

once more. The important thing, however, is that this latent enthusiasm is there – thanks to the club coaches.

Frowners and Brooders take note. What your game may need is a coaching session.

Not on grip.
Not on style.
On smiling.

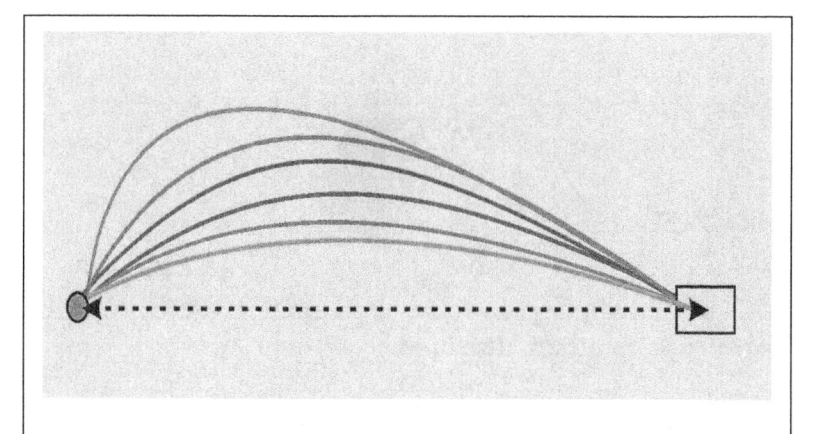

If there was a criticism of the coaching team's classroom sessions it was that their charts all too often bore little relation to reality.

BOWLSPEAK

BLOCKER

Bowl deliberately placed so as to make it difficult for the opposition to attack the head.

BLOODY BLOCKER

Bowl accidentally placed which makes it difficult for the culprit's own team to get anywhere near the head.

Bowls for the Bewildered

Every bowls club will have a dark and sad little corner – possibly a pretty big corner – with which new bowlers quickly become familiar.

Perhaps they've responded to an advertised "Come and Try" day. Or they've seen a sign on the club's gate saying that "New Members Are Welcome". Or they are Shruggers brought along by their bowling acquaintance with the mutual aims of shutting each other up.

Whichever it is, the new bowlers will almost certainly arrive *sans* bowls and need to put to the test the club's lofty claim that "all equipment is provided". And into the sad little corner they are led. It is the corner, of course, which contains the tatty sets of bowls with which the new recruits are expected to learn the game.

(Let us overlook the obvious point that this approach appears rather illogical: akin to Leonardo da Vinci welcoming a new group of students and, before starting his course on the finer points of painting, arming them with a loo brush. Perhaps the thinking is that if the new bowler can cope with learning how to play the game using a set of mismatched and antiquated bowls then they can cope with anything.) [18]

Fast forward. The new bowler has joined the club. They've played a few games, delving on each occasion into the sad little corner to retrieve the same tatty bowls they've grown familiar with. Dissatisfaction has begun to wind its tentacles around their heart. Before they know it they're comparing their borrowed club set against the

---

[18] Part of the problem is that many of the club's sets will have been owned by a now-deceased member. Whether they were donated by the late player's bowling soul-mate or, with relief, by a related Scoffer is immaterial. They will have a sentimental value that prevents them from being disposed of at the earliest opportunity.

sparkling new affairs being sported by the more established members they're playing alongside. They feel like an impoverished lodger rubbing shoulders with swanky home owners. Before they know it, the decision is made: they need to have their own set of bowls ...

And so begins a rite of passage comparable to buying one's first car. How to make the big decision? Research carefully, examine the options, study performances and compare prices – or just dive in with what looks to be a reasonable option and get it over and done with?

As with potential cars there is a bewildering amount of choice in bowls. Budget constraints might suggest a second-hand set. [19] The chances are, however, that this option may not feel much of a step up from plundering the club's tatty collection.

Moreover, and to alter the analogy to the search for a spouse / partner, there may well be lurking at the back of the bowler's mind the vague, rose-tinted notion that this could be a union for life. The right decision is vital.

Ultimately, that decision may well take into account all the most important variables: a nice feel, an attractive line, not too heavy to handle (the analogy is back to cars again, we hasten to add) but it's equally likely to be decided in much the same fashion: "I couldn't make up my mind, so in the end I went for the ones with the nicest colour!" [20]

---

[19] Or "pre-loved", if you can believe the advertiser. Best to examine for hatchet marks, though.

[20] Some bowlers hedge their bets here by owning more than one set of bowls. Ask why and you will most likely get a scientific explanation about different biases to cater for different playing conditions. Tosh. Either they're to be used much as a multi-putter golfer switches putters whenever the current one doesn't seem to be working, or they're of different colours. Probably both.

As with so many things in life, size matters

HUE AND CRY

When advertising the new-fangled Model T Ford back in 1908, Henry Ford told his sales managers, "Any customer can have a car painted in any colour he wants so long as it is black." Older players will remember the days when pretty much the same extensive choice applied to bowls.

This norm of black bowls (or a rather racy deep brown) was originally determined by the fact that they were made of a wood: lignum vita. Native to the Caribbean or South America, it's a wood which is strong, tough and dense. Ecological considerations, plus the insistence of the trees in growing incredibly slowly, mean that true 'woods' have been consigned to the ditch of history. [21]

Today's "composite" bowls – made from microwaved and shaped melamine granules – are not only amazing feats of technical progress but provide the one feature that true 'woods' lacked: variety of colour. The melamine granules can be dyed to any hue that the manufacturer thinks will sell. They are now regularly mixed with other coloured granules to produce the bowls equivalent of spotted dick – speckled bowls. And, for those who simply can't make up their mind, revolting two- and even four-coloured bowls are available. [22]

Buying a set of bowls, then, gives the player a chance to do more than purchase an essential piece of sporting equipment. It gives them the opportunity to *make a statement*.

"These bowls," the player is announcing to the world, "aren't just round things. They're telling you something about *me*."

The downside to statements made with highly-visible sets of bowls is, of course, that they are highly visible. Great when they're snuggled cosily against the jack, but not so hot when they're miles away and you'd prefer to be rather more anonymous. Then, as far the world is concerned, a rash of rather different statements can pop into mind …

---

[21] Bowlers who'd like to try a set of lignum vitae bowls should visit the most cobwebbed region of the sad corner in their club. An ancient set will almost certainly be found there.

[22] Coloured bowls have been available for many years, but spectators at big championships wouldn't have noticed. Until 1998 the authorities only permitted the use of black or brown bowls.

Atomic Red (Henselite)

You're Saying: Explosive performer
They're Thinking: Scattered like shrapnel

Iced Lime (Taylor)

You're Saying: Cool and calm
They're Thinking: Green and drippy

Harlequin (Drakes Pride)

You're Saying: Entertainer
They're Thinking: Clown

Confetti (Aero)

You're Saying: Celebrated
They're Thinking: Sprinkled everywhere

Picasso (Aero)

You're Saying: Artist
They're Thinking: What the hell is that supposed to be?

EMBLEMS

Older readers may remember that it was once all the fashion to have your bowls identified by your initials. This phase passed, [23] to be replaced either by choosing an image from the manufacturer's stock library or taking pot luck with whatever you were given.

These are still options. Again, though, technology has moved on. Manufacturers offer a choice from thousands of emblems. Or, to return to our car-buying analogy, buyers can add the equivalent of a personalised number plate and design one for themselves. Either way, going for an emblem that's too distinctive is as risky as opting

---

[23] If only because initials narrow the market terribly if you're trying to get rid of the things on Ebay.

for a garish colour. You might think that your emblem is saying one thing to the world but others might see it in an entirely different light ...

Emblem: Star

You're Saying: Bright
They're Thinking: Best seen with a telescope

Emblem: Question Mark

You're Saying: How did s/he do that so well?
They're Thinking: How did s/he do that so badly?

Emblem: Rocket

You're Saying: High-flyer
They're Thinking: Mostly in orbit

Emblem: Sign of the Zodiac

You're Saying: Predictable
They're Thinking: Unbelievable

Emblem: Bowls Player

You're Saying: That's me
They're Thinking: In your dreams

Emblem: Sports Equipment

You're Saying: I play other games
They're Thinking: I wish you would

Given all the above, bewildered bowls purchasers may decide that it would be best to shelter in the anonymity of conventional black.

Sadly, this is a diminishing option. With bowls greens looking ever more as though a tube of Smarties has been spilt on them, the black and brown bowls are beginning to stick out. Soon they'll be seen as the 'new' colours – and all the above statement and image provisos will apply to them as well.

What to do, then?

There's only one answer. Get your bowls, of whatever colour, closer to the jack.

Something about the owner's chosen wording suggested a marked lack of confidence.

NON-BOWLSPEAK

With bowls players having more hearing aids per head (literally) than most, gestures can play as important a role as the spoken word. Viewed from the mat ...

HAND WAVING FROM SIDE TO SIDE

The last bowl is roughly level with the jack – albeit in the next rink.

HANDS APART

Approximate, but gratifyingly short, distance of last bowl from the jack.

FLAT HAND SOMEWHERE ABOVE GROUND

Still approximate, but greater than short, distance of last bowl from the jack.

FLAT HAND ABOVE HEAD, OCCASIONALLY WITH JUMPING ACTION

Forget approximations. Last bowl is miles from the jack.

FLAT HAND POINTING DOWNWARDS

Indication of where the jack is. Helpful if it's hidden, but very sarcastic if it's in full view. And very, very sarcastic if no bowls have yet been delivered.

Top (and Bottom) Gear

Like many sports, bowls has a dress code. Football teams, for example, have a dress code which changes every twelve months so as to maximise revenue from gullible fans who simply must have an up-to-date replica shirt. It's a dress code, moreover, which changes depending on whether the team is playing at home or away.

The dress code for bowls is also a moveable feast, but with the difference that what the bowler wears doesn't so much depend on where they're playing, but in what sort of game. The only thing you can pretty much guarantee is that you're never going to appear in the buff. [24]

The reason is essentially administrative. "No man is an island," wrote John Donne in 1624, and the same goes for bowls clubs. They will almost certainly be affiliated to a district bowls association; and, in the UK, a county bowls association and the national bowls association – each of which will run competitions and specify a dress code for those taking part in them.

If this sounds like a hierarchy then that's because it is. Districts and counties may be permitted to have their own little variations, but ultimately it is the national association which owns primacy of the sport's dress code. Think of it as similar to being a member of the EU and subject to EU law – but with no possibility of an in/out referendum.

---

[24] Not 100% true. In 2019, after former Under-25 international Hannah Overton had been diagnosed with (and, aged 29, subsequently died from) acute myeloid leukaemia, a number of our top bowls players and administrators stripped off for the *Hot Shots of Bowls 2019 Calendar* in support of the charities *Cancer Research UK* and *Bloodwise*. Sponsored by magazine *Bowls International*, it's now a collector's item. Those who set out to track one down in the hope of glimpsing a displaced kitty or two are doomed to disappointment, though. The photographers were all experts at covering shots.

This isn't as bad, or as arcane, as it sounds. Bowls clubs can devise their own rules for the club's internal events. But if players are representing their club – or, higher up the tree, their county – or, even higher up the tree, appearing in a prestigious national final, then it's not unreasonable to say that they can't just arrive wearing the outfit they picked up for a song during their holiday in Bermuda.

WAIST NOT, WANT NOT

Bowls dress codes also have a certain olde-worlde charm about them - in particular, their use of the delightfully quaint phrases "above the waist" (ATW) and "below the waist" (BTW).

The implied assumption here, of course, is that the bowler attempting to follow the code has a waist that can be located with some degree of certainty. A look at any busy bowling green is all that's needed to see that this is not so. Bowls may well be a game for all ages, but it's also a game for all girths.

Younger bowlers may indeed have a clearly discernible waist, but for those of more mature years 'waist' is not so much a line of latitude as an equatorial region that can extend either north or south of the navel – sometimes both. For the bewildered, then, a simple rule of thumb is:
- If the item is pulled down to be put on and pulled up to be taken off then it's above the waist (e.g. hats and shirts)
- If it's pulled up to be put on and pulled down to be taken off then it's below the waist (e.g. shoes, socks and items covering the nether regions)

Let's look at the dress code for each of these in turn – from head to toe, as one might say.

ATW: Hats (aka Headwear)

Hats can be white or of a colour which is consistent with the shirt beneath it. But, for the fashion-conscious bowler, conforming with the dress code is the easy bit. Finding headwear that suits is another matter entirely. The choice is between the functional and the stylish.

- Baseball Cap. Functional, but clearly a confusing item for younger bowlers who never seem able to work out which way round it goes.
- Coal Scuttle / Bucket. Seriously un-stylish, but no possibility of getting it the wrong way round.
- Flat Cap. Functional, masculine. Could come back into fashion one day. But then so could spats.
- Wide-brimmed and in various styles for both men and women. Both functional and, usually, stylish. Difficult to deal with in a strong wind, though. The choice is often between an un-stylish chin strap or the possibility of an embarrassed pursuit across the green.

ATW: Shirt

Gone are the days when male bowlers were required to wear a collar and tie, whilst ladies had to dress as though they were off to a wedding.

Nowadays, both now wear the same type of garment: a unisex club shirt. The design of this shirt has to be approved by a higher authority; clubs cannot decide unilaterally to adopt an article better suited to a jockey, or a psychedelic mixture of colours that could cause an epileptic fit. Once this hurdle has been cleared, this shirt is likely to become the most-worn item in the bowler's wardrobe.

League game, knock-out competition or friendly, if the bowler is representing their club, then on will go the

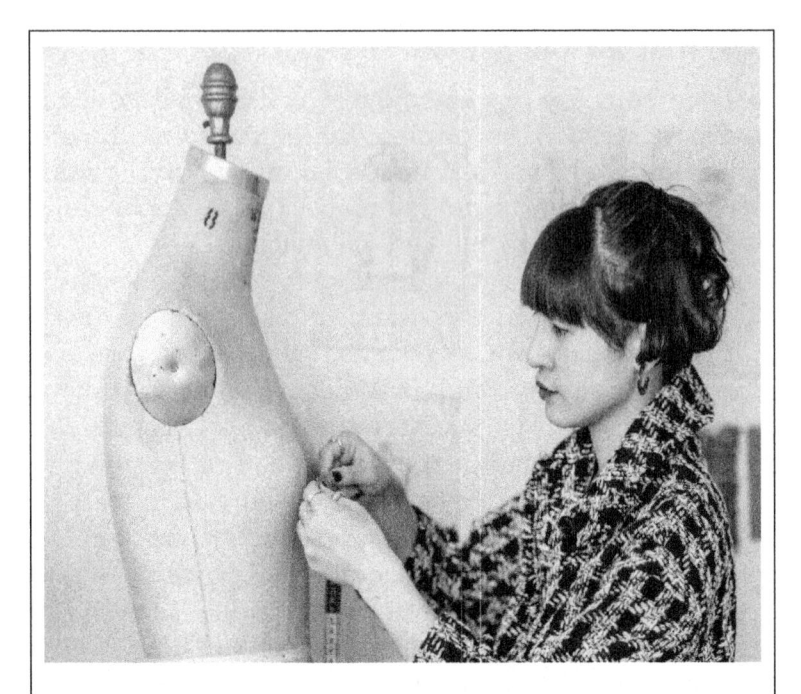

She understood the reason for having to wear a club shirt for matches, but was damned if she was going to put up with a 'one size fits nobody' monstrosity

shirt. Some clubs even demand that the shirt be worn for internal club competitions. The implications are clear:
- Fashion-conscious bowlers should check out the shirt design of any club they're thinking of joining. It's bad enough being a Frowner on the green without falling prey to the affliction in the changing room as well
- It's a good idea to have more than one shirt. The "wear one, spare one, one in the wash" is a sound principle to follow. Games can come thick and fast during the season and a shirt that heralds your arrival before you've come through the front gate is not a good idea.

BTW: Shoes (and Socks)

We've arrived at the one item in the dress code which gives the flamboyant bowler an opportunity to set themselves apart from the crowd – and it's not the socks. The rules say that socks, if seen, should be white. If not seen, they can be purple with pink spots but as they can't be seen there's not a great deal of point in wearing them. No, the loophole for the would-be Flash Harry or the Flashier Harriette is with their shoes. All the dress code has to say about them is that
    (a) They have to be worn
    (b) They have to be 'flat-soled' (but not sandals - unless you've got a doctor's note). [25]
Not a dicky-bird, then, about permissible colour(s). Bowls gear manufacturers have been slow to cotton on to this, but they're catching up fast: it's now possible to buy shoes in a variety of colours; that are two-toned; with a flashy flash – or all three. It's surely only a matter of time before colour-matched bowls and shoes hit the market. You read it here first.

BTW: Nether Regions Coverage

Finally, we come to the coverage of that area between the waistline (wherever that may be) and the ankles. Here the dress code has changed markedly. [26]

---

[25] See the *Bowls Hot-Shots of 2019 Calendar* mentioned previously. Birthday-suited they may have been, but below the ankles every single player was sporting correct and impeccably-soled footwear.

[26] Note that the dress code, as yet, doesn't mention underwear. At one point, though, it stipulates that items should be of an *opaque* (i.e. non-see-through) material. Given the amount of bending down that the game involves, this is sensible. Ladies and gentlemen can thus wear their lucky tiger-print thongs and boxer shorts (or vice-versa) without fear of startling the spectators whenever they play a shot.

Bowls has recently gone down cricket's gaudy path, allowing below-the-waist-wear that's consistent in colour with the shirts above. However, as these all have to be the same shade, and not just any old rough match, it's still the case that grey and 'predominantly white' are the dress code's prescribed colours. So far, so good.

Matters then become a little more complicated. Ladies in particular have a bewildering choice. Skirts, culottes, tailored full-length trousers or tailored cropped trousers are all allowed. In these days of equality it's difficult to say what the reaction would be if a gentleman turned out in any of these options, but if they prefer to play it safe then trousers are the conventional choice.

However, in recent years a further possibility has been added to the code: having been outlawed for years, bowls players may now wear shorts.

Not any old shorts, mark you. They have to be tailored, approved and moreover, *licensed*, by the national body. This is controversial for two reasons.

Firstly, the code appears to be saying that playing in shorts is only legal if the body passing the law is making money out of it. This is like the government saying that it's perfectly legal to get yourself blind drunk so long as they're receiving a cut of the price of your alcohol. Oh, they do. It's called a tax.

Secondly – traditionalists would argue - the rule is faintly perverse. The whole *raison d'être* for a dress code is surely to define a minimum standard of appearance. And yet now, a rule that insists on a uniformity of decorum in most areas, permits the exposure of legs: legs that, at one end of the scale, may not have been seen in daylight for the best part of forty years and, at the other, be so heavily tattooed that they could easily be mistaken for a couple of rolls of wallpaper.

And as for the knobbly knees …

"Bugger the Armada! What do you mean, I can't play in shorts unless they've got a Bowles Englande logo on them?"

NON-BOWLSPEAK continued

It's generally thought useful to let the bowler on the mat know what the position is at the head, score-wise. This information can be bellowed, and might be if the position is good, but it's usually conveyed by sign language. Thus:

TAPPING SHOULDER x TIMES

Bowler's side are currently holding x shots

(sub-text: "so don't cock things up").

TAPPING LEG x TIMES

Player's side are currently down by x shots

(sub-text "so join the game and *do* something").

That concludes our examples of non-bowlspeak.

This is not to say that no other gestures might be seen during a bowls match. A variety may well be. However, these will often convey emotion rather than information.

When in doubt, study the reaction of the bowler on the receiving end of the gesture.

Playin' In The Rain

> *I'm playin' in the rain*
> *Just playin' in the rain*
> *What a miserable feeling*
> *I'm soaked yet again*
> *I'm cursing the clouds*
> *Peeing down from above*
> *Every crevice is damp*
> *This ain't weather I love ...* [27]

It's a fallacy to suggest that bowls is only played in good weather. It isn't. It's an all-weather game, played come rain or shine. (Clearly this doesn't apply to bowlers who never venture outdoors. Unless their indoor club has an exceptionally leaky roof they can skip this chapter).

This is not to say that bowlers enjoy playing in rain. The stuff can and does cause all sort of problems – and, for those with a Shaker-cum-Scoffer at home, not only on the green.

When the sun is shining, the Shaker mood will be in the ascendant. "S/he's out in the fresh air," will go their train of thought, "boosting their levels of vitamin D3 with all its attendant benefits of strengthened bone structure, improved heart function and heightened immune system. Plus, I can go and have a nice laze in the garden while s/he's out."

Introduce some glowering clouds and a warning of hailstorms, though, and this mood is likely to darken with the weather. The Scoffer will be back and asking, "You're

---

[27] With apologies to the spirit of Arthur Freed, lyricist for *Singin' In The Rain (1929)*.

going to play bowls in *this*?", repeating for emphasis and adding capitals, "in THIS?"

And, if truth be told, even the most fanatical bowler will struggle to come up a decent reason as to why they're proposing to do just that.

Playing in the rain may sometimes be necessary – unavoidable if the rain arrives half-way through a game which started when there wasn't a cloud in the sky – but it's never fun. Find a bowler who claims to enjoy playing in a downpour and you've found one who's likely to have Pinocchio in their family tree. Watch them very carefully when they're measuring.

The problems can be summarised in two words: comfort and control. Bowlers at whatever level need to stand on the mat feeling comfortable. If that's not so, then the essential element of controlling their bowl becomes even harder than usual. To do both when the heavens open is a serious challenge.

Comfort first. Regular swimmers may be happy to play on regardless, their clothing way beyond saturation point. [28] The vast majority of bowlers, however, invest in what is laughingly known as 'wet-weather gear': that is, supposedly waterproof hats, jackets and trousers.

Hats are not so bad. They can be removed, given a shake, then quickly put back on again. It's the jackets and trousers which cause more of a problem.

When it comes to rainfall, all bowlers seem to be unfailingly optimistic. Trusting that it's just a shower and that the sun will soon come out, they invariably pile their wet-weather gear on top of everything else.

This tactic is doubly bad for comfort. Firstly, the added layers inevitably restrict movement. More import-

---

[28] But may, thereby, be in serious breach of the dress code. As 'wet T-shirt' contests are designed to exploit, opaque cladding for the nether regions can become awfully non-opaque when soaked.

It certainly passed the style test, but would it keep the rain off?

antly, as all the 'how to avoid hypothermia and/or reduce your heating bills' leaflets tell us, multiple layers trap body heat. Body heat leads to perspiration – and the irony is that clothing advertised as being just what you need to keep moisture out seems to be even more effective at keeping the stuff in. Prolonged spells of rain will have the bowler feeling as though they've wandered fully-clothed into a sauna.

And, after all this, the weather will probably still win. Raindrops are like gnats. Cover up all you will, the little devils will still find a way in somewhere.

Now control. Assuming the bowler can cope with the discomfort of feeling like a wet rag both inside and out, how do they prevent the bowl from squirting out of their hand like a bar of soap in the shower? A twin-pronged approach is the usual answer: dry the bowl and increase the gripping power of the hands.

Bowlers are thus advised to equip themselves with dry cloths by the dozen. (How these are kept dry until needed is left as an exercise for the reader).

As for the hands, a glove is often a favoured option. For those players who like to 'feel' the bowl and liken wearing a glove to paddling with your socks on, the answer is to cover the delivery hand with some sort of gripping agent. 'Grippo'™ – a kind of non-permanent glue – is the market leader in this regard, although more imaginative solutions can be effective. Tony Allcock, former world outdoor and indoor singles champion, has said (*Bowls International, June '22*) that a light coating of furniture polish often did the trick for him. [29]

Ultimately, there may be only one thing that can be offered in support of playing bowls in a deluge: *Laws of the Sport of Bowls, rules 33.1, 33.1.3 and 33.2* – and even they depend on your point of view.

These rules state:

33.1 If a game is stopped because of ... weather conditions ... by ...

33.1.3 ... agreement between the players ... the game must be continued on the same day or on a different day ...

---

[29] Sadly, the article doesn't say whether the former champion was also in the habit of preventing mugs slipping off his coffee table by giving it a quick once-over with 'Grippo'.

33.2 If an end has started but all the required bowls have not been played, it must be declared dead. (The end <u>must be declared dead</u> even if one or more players choose to remain on the green during the stoppage.)

The implications are obvious. When in a tight match with a crucial end going badly, the bowler's tactics must be to (a) pray for rain (b) hope their opponent agrees to a stoppage (c) hope also that they don't know rule 33.2 and, finally, (d) hope that they can find their rule book so as to point this out before the rain stops.

The green's moisture-retention properties meant that, for the benefit of shorter members, matches sometimes had to be played over 18 or 21 shallow ends.

BOWLSPEAK

UNPLAYABLE GREEN (1)

Green that has become saturated. The usual signs are:

* Water oozing from the surface when the bowler steps onto the green – temporary unplayability
* Green below water – longer term unplayability
* Player below water – indoor rink laid above a swimming pool has problems with subsidence

UNPLAYABLE GREEN (2)

Playing surface so poorly maintained that it's virtually impossible, even for a champion, to get a bowl to behave as it's supposed to.

UNPLAYABLE GREEN (3)

Figment of the bowler's imagination, especially after they have been on the receiving end of a drubbing.

Chalk Talk

Here's an idea for a new TV game show. It's working title is *Bag A Fortune*. Every week a professional crook lifts a bag or suitcase while its owner's not looking. One week it may be a case snaffled from the baggage carousel at Heathrow, another a bag parted from its unwary owner in Harrods. And the idea is not that the crook has to deliver the bag to the TV studios before they're caught by the police. The possibility of failure is an essential ingredient to keep an audience interested.

No, when the bag reaches the TV studio it's opened and – before being returned to its rightful owner – a contestant has to guess which of the items inside is the most valuable. Get it right and they bag a fortune (to be defined).

It sounds perfect for Ant and Dec to host on a Saturday night. Audience numbers could set new records, and not only amongst those anxious to keep up to date with the latest in pilfering techniques pending their release from His Majesty's Pleasure. A viewing public with a track record of watching (or, at the very least, fast-forwarding) untold hours of *Big Brother* and *Love Island* in the hope of spotting a wardrobe malfunction surely won't be able to resist the chance of a nose into an innocent victim's luggage. It's got 'winner' stamped all over it.

Bowlers, of course, will be too busy bowling – until the trailer for the coming week lets slip that a bowls bag is going to put in an appearance. [30] When that happens, viewing figures will go through the roof.

---

[30] Bowls expenditure is a slippery slope. Having acquired bowls, shoes etc. it's inevitable that the bowler will need something to carry them in. Turning up at the club with your equipment in a pillow case slung over your shoulder is unseemly.

The contestant will be introduced amidst some chirpy badinage from the hosts. The bag will then be wheeled in and hefted on to a table. Slowly, its contents will be taken out for the contestant to assess.

Bowls – possibly new and shiny. Shoes – perhaps a little down at the heel. Waterproof jacket and trousers. Microlite cloth in some luminous colour. And then, to a ripple of audience excitement, a wrinkled and aged copy of the *Rules of the Sport of Bowls*. Could it be a valuable first edition? ask our hosts. They check inside the front cover and are disappointed not to find 'property of Sir F. Drake' scrawled inside. A recent copy, they conclude, its pages wrinkled and faded due to having been used as a shoe tree once too often.

Finally, a tiny aerosol canister is fished out. 'Spray chalk' it is says on the side. The contestant looks flummoxed. What's it for? Do you want to phone a friend? offer our chirpy hosts. The contestant does.

We hear a phone ringing, once, twice. And then, amazingly, it's answered. The friend doesn't have a call guardian system filtering out random calls from unknown sources such as scammers and TV studios; the friend isn't in the shower; the friend isn't even on hold with a help desk that's telling them their call is important but all their agents are busy right now. The friend is available to talk.

The contestant has made a wise choice of friend. When asked what a bowler's spray chalk is for, the answer is not: "Sorry, haven't got a bloody clue."

No, the friend is knowledgeable. It's used for marking touchers, explains the friend, a toucher being a bowl which touches the jack at some point in its travels. The mark is to indicate that should the bowl subsequently get knocked into the ditch then it remains 'live' and in play.

The contestant looks grateful. Ant and Dec look smug, as if they knew all that. If there's a little bit of time to kill before the next commercial break they might even let the friend say more. A chalk mark on a toucher, we would hear, is not necessarily a badge of merit. A perfect bowl which ends up nestled lovingly against the jack gets exactly the same squirt of chalk as a bowl which gives the jack the most perfunctory of kisses before continuing its journey into the wilderness.

"Yeah, right," says the contestant finally. The hosts say it's time for the big decision: what is the most valuable item in the bowls bag? The contestant umms and ahhs and tries to sound intelligent - then plumps for the Armani wet-weather jacket with the faint smell of mildew.

Wrong, wrong, wrong.

The last we see and hear of this hapless soul as they leave empty-handed is a wan smile and a sympathetic round of applause.

The above was, admittedly, a roundabout way of pointing out that spray chalk is extremely expensive.

It used to be the case that a bowler could buy a box of 20 sticks of blackboard chalk on the day they took up the game and still have some left to bequeath in their will. As a modern alternative, the literate bowler could invest in a chalk pen; this would also last a good time.

Both have fallen out of favour. Their common disadvantage is that in order to use them to mark a toucher the bowl, ironically, has to be touched – with the attendant risk of the bowl accidentally (never deliberately!) being moved. A puff with a chalk spray is like a pair of luvvies air-kissing on the red carpet at the Oscars: no contact is needed at all.

The down side is the cost. At the time of writing, a 10g canister of spray chalk will relieve the bowler of £4.50 or thereabouts. Money for weight, that puts the stuff in the same league as Dom Perignon champagne and Chanel No.5 perfume – without tasting anything like as nice or smelling as good.

> It wasn't a large room, just big enough to hold the club's trophies and supplies of puffer chalk

On the extortion ladder it's probably only a rung or two below the thimbleful of ink put into printer cartridges before they're sold for almost as much as their host printer cost in the first place.

To be fair, it's not all bad news though. On the positive side, spray chalks have pretty much done away with the tiresome antics of the 'chalk-wag'.

For the uninitiated, a chalk-wag is a bowler for whom putting a simple cross on a toucher is never enough – especially after a teammate has suffered something of a toucher drought. When the drought is finally broken, the chalk-wag will scatter so many x's on the successful bowl that it ends up looking like a Valentine's card.

Alternatives are jokey exclamations, such as "Yay!" or "Wow!" Checking their watches and inscribing the time is not unknown – and, if the drought has been particularly prolonged, adding the date. Extending this to include the year is very wounding.

Spray chalks have pretty much put a stop to all these shenanigans. Now, even the most dedicated chalk-wag will think twice about authenticating a toucher with their signature when they know that doing so will cost them an arm and a leg.

So a toucher in the ditch *was* something of a rarity, but the point could have been made with a little more subtlety.

BOWLSPEAK

WIN

An unmitigated triumph, all down to the bowler's talent.

Synonyms: victory, conquest, success ... *ad nauseam*

DRAW

A win by another name.

LOSE

A negative win.

When asked about such a game, the bowler's response will depend on the scale of the negativity:

1-5 shots: a definite win if the opposition hadn't had 1-5 outrageous breaks go their way

6 – 10 shots: staged a brave recovery following a series of 5-9 outrageous breaks until the opposition got yet another one on the last end

10+ shots: what game?

Line, Length and Condoms

Gladys is on her knees, praying.
"Lord, I'm up to my ears in debt. Please, let me win the lottery."
A week later, she's back in church again. "Lord, things are even worse. The phone has been cut off and the house is about to be repossessed. Let me win the lottery!"
As is always the way in stories like this, another week goes by and she's back for a third time.
"Lord, I'm at the end of my tether. I can't even afford my bowls club membership fee. I'm begging you. Let me win the lottery."
At this, lightning flashes and a voice booms down from heaven:
"Gladys, help me out here. Buy a lottery ticket!"

Bear with me. The point of that story will hopefully become clear at the end of this little essay.

It's an old bowler's saw (or sore) that success on the green requires the three L's – Line, Length and Luck.

The first two are surely indisputable. For a bowl to curve its way unerringly to its intended target requires it to be dispatched in the right direction to begin with. Direction, however, is insufficient on its own. It also has to stop on the right length – not too long and not too short, as Goldilocks might have said if she'd been a bowler..

But as an end progresses, matters can get increasingly complicated. What was the correct line and length when the path to the jack was open may have been rendered impossible by a collection of irritating bowls in the way. The desired line and length is now either going to be akin to threading a needle or, equally likely, involve some deliberate and quite possibly violent contact with the said irritants. This is where the 'luck' part is most likely to put in an appearance. But if in such a situation the delivered bowl proceeds to hit another, turn through a right angle, and finally end up nuzzling an astonished jack, is 'luck' really the right word to describe what's just happened?

Luck, good or bad, suggests that the end result is all down to pure chance rather than the player's own actions. Winning the lottery clearly fits the bill here. But for bowls? It's not a new question, by any means. Some of the biggest bananas in the literary world have referred to it.

Walter Scott, for one, back in 1824. In his novel *Redgauntlet* the hero, law student Darsie Latimer, has a conversation with a servant named Cristal Nixon – who may be a humble menial but is clearly familiar with the subtleties of our game.

"And how it fails?" said Darsie.
"Thereafter as it may be –" said Nixon, "they who play at bowls must meet with rubbers." (III vi)

(Readers who are also worldly-wise students of history may see a possible ambiguity here, since it was in the 1800's that 'rubbers' entered the lexicon as a slang term for condoms. A gentle reminder about bowls club demographics should dispel any idea that Scott was suggesting the possibility of a bowl being diverted from its path by a condom. Then, as now, the average age of a bowls clubs' lady members would be such as to render the use of such articles far from essential. As for elderly male members, it's common knowledge that they can be extraordinarily difficult to locate – even by their owners.)

To continue. We can remove any possible ambiguity by going back a further sixty years, to 1762, and a weird collection of tales written by Tobias Smollet entitled *The Life and Adventures of Sir Launcelot Greaves*. This book, predating any unseemly slang, includes one of those summary chapter headers popular at the time:

> "Which sheweth that he who plays at bowls will sometimes meet with rubbers." (I x)

Finally we can turn, as ever, to William Shakespeare. In his play, *Richard II*, a glum Queen is looking for a pick-me-up. She asks her lady-in-waiting:

QUEEN: What sport shall we devise here in this garden / To drive away the heavy thoughts of care?
LADY: Madam, we'll play at bowls.
QUEEN: 'Twill make me think the world is full of rubs / And that my fortune runs against the bias.

Now Shakespeare could have had the Queen (a Brooder if ever there was one) say she'll have bad luck. Nobody could dispute that our William knew plenty of words and 'luck' was one of them. He uses it (as well as 'lucky' and 'luckier') well over 20 times in various plays. The fact that he doesn't when talking about bowls suggests that his considerable brain saw subtle differences between luck and – to return to the traditional term for wicks, glides and the rest – rubs of the green.

Differences such as ... they're zero-sum, for starters. Gamble at roulette and it's perfectly possible for 'luck' to determine that every player loses their money. [31] Not in bowls. One player's fortunate rub spells a misfortunate one for the opposition.

Moreover, what tips the balance either way can be miniscule. The slightest of alterations in line or length and the rub can go the other way. To avoid it there would have to be major differences – differences sufficient to cause the bowl to miss the crucial area of the head altogether.

---

[31] The casino owners win, of course, but they're not playing bowls.

In other words, rubs of the green – good or bad – can usually only come about if the bowl is delivered to pretty much the right area in the first place.

As The Almighty could have told Gladys at the end of our opening story, "You've got to be in it to win it."

An updated three L's of success, then: Line, Length ... and Lots of rubs of the green.

Unconvinced that rubs of the green even out over the season, the squad buckled down to some serious winter training.

Do Unto Others ...

For a language which proudly states that it's not French, English has snaffled a fair few *bon mots* from it. "Nuance" has already been mentioned. Now it's the turn of the often misunderstood, "Etiquette".

Derived from the name given to little cards instructing French soldiers how to behave when billeted on poor, unsuspecting peasants, etiquette is commonly taken to mean a set of informal, unwritten rules governing polite behaviour in society.

For example, it was once accepted that a man would open a door for a woman. Do that today and the poor sap is likely to be told, "I'm not bleedin' helpless, y'know!"

This is the problem. Etiquette doesn't stand still. What is considered correct behaviour today, can get you a slap round the face tomorrow.

Bowls etiquette is no different. Acceptable behaviour on – and, occasionally, off – the green can be something of a moving target. One bowlers' polite behaviour can be another's "Yer what? Loosen up!"

What follows, then, is simply a brief starter list of what is, and is not, sound bowls-playing etiquette as of today. It could well change tomorrow. [32]

BEFORE THE GAME

It is customary to acknowledge one's opponents. Pre-pandemic, this was always by means of a handshake. Etiquette could now have morphed for either party into a fist-bump or an elbow-nudge. The problem is, there's no way of knowing which your opponent prefers. You simply

---

[32] A useful rule of thumb is the proverb, "Do unto others as you would have them do unto you." Beware, though. It has its limitations. Bowlers who may be happy to have their backside tickled during delivery could well find that their personal code of etiquette is not reciprocated.

have to accept that there's a good chance of the game beginning with a confusion of shaken elbows or elbowed fists.

**Were they really unaware that a
pre-match handshake was sufficient
or were they being wilfully obtuse?**

DURING THE GAME

Extra care is needed during the actual hostilities. Never assume that bonhomie in the clubhouse will survive the journey to the green.

- When an opponent is on the mat, don't speak or clatter loose bowls together - ideally, don't make any sound at all. Players whose hearing can be sadly deficient when they're asked to stump up their green fees can suddenly find themselves capable of hearing a butterfly land on a petal.
- Similarly, don't move a muscle. It's not unknown for a player whose performance is suggesting that they're having trouble seeing the jack to be found to have eyes in the back of their head.
- A good shot, on the other hand, should always be complimented. "Well bowled" is the usual formula of words. [33] Now it has to be admitted that, in a hard-fought and nail-bitingly close game, even the most generous Smiler might find themselves muttering this plaudit through clenched teeth. For those hoping to play seriously competitive stuff, an evening class in ventriloquism is recommended.
- Should you play a shot that receives a "well bowled" – sincere or otherwise – acknowledge it modestly. "Thank you," is the standard response. To shrug and say, "Piece of cake" is not only poor etiquette but a hostage to fortune; it may turn out to be the only good shot you play all game.

---

[33] A host of others may spring to mind, but good etiquette demands that that is where they must stay.

Mona was never less than a gracious opponent, but the smug look on her face whenever she drew shot was really bloody irritating.

AFTER THE GAME

Win, lose or draw, etiquette continues to apply:

- Go through the handshake/fist-bump/elbow routine again. The chances are that you'll all remember the confusion before the game and change your approach – thereby causing a

different collection of shaken elbows and elbowed fists.
- Thank your opponents for an enjoyable game. (Ventriloquistic skills may apply here also).
- If playing at home, offer to buy your opposite number a drink. This can be tricky if you've left home without any cash. In that case plan B is to add a hopeful, "Unless you've got to dash, the traffic can be terrible if you leave it much later than this ..." Should that fail, plan C is to use the green fees you've wisely kept in your pocket and settle up with the treasurer later.
- If playing away, always accept the offered drink. It's only good etiquette, after all.

They may have lost on the green, but they wiped the floor with them in the bar afterwards.

BOWLSPEAK

CALLING THROUGH

The practice of encouraging an opponent's bowl to carry on running further than they intended. This is seriously bad etiquette and exceptionally unsporting; behaviour that is only exceeded by laughing when their bowl does precisely what you wanted.

"BAD LUCK"

Commiseration offered to one's opponent when their shot – which you sportingly refrained from calling through and didn't laugh about when it did precisely what you wanted – finally comes to a halt.

Related phrases: One shot to me, then.

Roll-Up, Roll-Up, Get Your Excuses Here!

To a smoker – those social pariahs nowadays banished to distant corners of the earth where they can indulge in their nasty habit with each other – a roll-up is a self-made cigarette; a sort of unkempt, raggedy version of the perfectly cylindrical fags on sale, at enormous expense, in cellophane-wrapped packs emblazoned with their dire health warnings.

Bowls club roll-ups are similar: the unkempt, raggedy bit that is, not that they should carry a health warning. In one way they're not unlike that first, sneaked cigarette: a rite of passage. New bowlers, fresh from their coaching induction sessions, will often gain their initial, spluttering experiences of the game – and of other bowlers – from club roll-ups. [34]

The principle at work here is that players looking for a game simply turn up (roll up) at a prescribed time, are formed into teams, and proceed to play. The event can be organised or not. Often it's difficult to tell the difference.

What cannot be understated is that the business of forming teams to play is both central and anything but straightforward. It's not simply a matter of tossing car keys into a bucket and drawing them out. This may have worked for the sort of dinner parties that used to be described in the disgraced *News of the World* before the reporter (always male) made his excuses and left, but a bowls roll-up is far more complicated. Players have to be allocated to (a) a rink, (b) a team and – most important of all – (c) a playing position within the team.

A typical, low-tech, method for achieving this is to have all roll-uppers draw a token which has each of these three elements inscribed on it. Thus informed, players

---

[34] Some might argue that this means the similarities should indeed be extended to include health warnings.

head off to their nominated rink. There, they discover who their teammates are to be. For the sake of argument, let's assume that each of the teams is a 'Four' – that is, a team comprising Lead, Two, Three and Skip.

(The subtleties of playing as a member of a Four are covered in more detail elsewhere. For now, the novice is asked to assume that the later one plays in sequence, the greater the carnage ahead.)

If things have worked out then, each of the roll-up teams should have somebody with a token stating which of the four positions they've drawn to play in. Now the fun starts ...

SKIP: Does anybody want to be Skip?
TWO: I'll do it if nobody else wants to. Who'll be Two?
LEAD: I prefer playing Three. Anybody want to be Lead?
THREE: Not me. I'm happy where I am. Three or Skip suits me.
SKIP: I don't like playing Lead. I'm best at Two or Three.
TWO: Am I Skip, then? .
THREE: You or me, by the look of it.

... At which point the team discovers that the negotiations have given it two Skips, three Threes, a Two and no Leads.

Change of analogy. For new bowlers, a roll-up (once play finally begins) can also be likened to that first solo taking to the road after passing the driving test. You know all the theory, you've been taught the way to do things correctly, you've taken mini-outings with your instructor in the safe environment of a dual-control car – and now, suddenly, you find yourself pitched into the bowls equivalent of the

Sorting out the roll-up teams was taking so long that extreme measures were called for.

M25 with a motley collection of hot-rods, sedate saloons and old bangers.

It's a learning experience, which is why ignoring the tokens saying who's going to play where is unfortunate. Every position in a bowls team is different. Roll-ups provide an unthreatening opportunity for bowlers to try the different shots that different positions demand.

To play different shots inevitably means discovering different ways of failing, of course. Now there are only two ways of dealing with failure: admit to a lack of talent ... or come up with an excuse – ideally, an excuse which shows that the failure was only apparent and was really a success in disguise. [35]

This is where the club roll-up has no equal for new bowlers. Building up a good repertoire of excuses takes time, and in no other arena are they likely to meet players with as much experience and creativity. Never join a roll-up without a notebook and/or your mobile phone set to 'record'.

Sadly, in a short essay such as this, it's impossible to do true justice to the subject of the bowls excuse. What follows, then, can only give the reader a flavour. This may be no bad thing. Bowls excuses are a bit like hair styles (some readers may have to exercise their long-term memories here). You see one you like and either try to copy it, adapt it to the raw material at your disposal, or see that it makes other people laugh and resolve to give it a miss. In other words, excuses are a matter of personal choice. [36]

Those that follow, therefore, are generic and linked to playing as a member of a Four. (Adapt as necessary for Triples and Pairs. [37]) They're really no more than starter excuses, heard during any club roll-up. Take them, style

---

[35] Smilers have a head start over Frowners here, because the essence of the perfect excuse for a dodgy shot is in spotting something – nay, anything – positive to say about it. Thinking dark thoughts about what went wrong makes good excuse formulation almost impossible.

[36] A word of warning. Although highly appropriate, bowlers are advised to never, ever use the phrase 'error of judgement'. To do so will land them in some very unsavoury company. The phrase has been commandeered by the many public figures who delight in telling us to do one thing whilst they do the opposite. When found out, they're not guilty of hypocrisy, oh no, but an 'error of judgement'. Bowlers' excuses may challenge credulity but never by that much.

[37] Coming up with plausible excuses when playing singles requires the bowler to be both a creative genius and a complete idiot. Difficult, but not impossible.

them, add some vivid colouring or wild and rambling extensions. Or play the game better.

LEAD

Shot played: short/medium/ long jack ...

Excuse: "I thought it was time we had <whatever length of jack was actually delivered>"

Shots played: both deliveries left miles away from jack ...

Excuse: (To TWO) "Notice I've left you plenty of room"

TWO

Shot played: Lead's rare toucher knocked off the jack and replaced by their own bowl ...

Excuse: "You're behind now. Far better position."

Shot played: both deliveries into outer space ...

Excuse: (To THREE) "I've anticipated where the covering bowls should go. You can just draw now."

THREE

Shot played: Opponent's bowl promoted to shot ...

Excuse: "It was in my way where it was."

Shot played: Bowl falling miles short of the head ...

Excuse: (To LEAD and TWO) "Skip's going to appreciate that blocker."

Shot played: Rocket into the end ditch after being asked to provide a back bowl ...

Excuse: (To SKIP) "That should give you an idea of the weight you need."

SKIP

Before playing a shot ...

Excuse: "It looks tricky, but I'll do the best I can."

Shot played: any ...

Excuse: : "Pretty good, considering how tricky it was."

Even the most gullible roll-uppers didn't buy the attempt to link an exhibition of wayward firing to the need for improved ventilation in the clubhouse

Skips Ahoy!

One doesn't have to be a member of a bowls club for very long – a few minutes, perhaps – before a quivering finger points in the direction of an imperious-looking individual and the newcomer is told in breathless tones, "He / She / That is a SKIP."

Now, depending on how new the member is, this word may mean nothing. It may even conjure up all sorts of entertaining images – 'skip' being a word with multiple meanings, such as:

- Jump up and down in one place
  (not wholly irrelevant, as it happens)
- Avoid something unwanted
  (ditto)
- Quickly go from one thing to another
  (double ditto)
- A large container for unwanted objects
  (wishful thinking by non-skips)

However, if the new member is sharp enough to work out that 'skip' is an abbreviation of 'skipper' – a nautical synonym for 'captain' – and, in addition, knows their poetry, a little ditty penned by Walt Whitman in 1865 might well spring to mind instead:

> *O Captain! my Captain! our fearful trip is done,*
> *The ship has weather'd every rack,*
> *the prize we sought is won,*
> *The port is near, the bells I hear,*
> *the people all exulting ...*

Images of skips having rose petals strewn at their feet, or being carried from the green on the shoulders of grateful teammates, could then quickly follow – until, if the new member really knows their poetry, they remember the final lines of the stanza:

> ... Where on the deck my Captain lies,
> Fallen cold and dead. [38]

Yes, being a skip is a double-edged sword. For some bowlers it is a position keenly sought: they imagine themselves as some future hero(ine) of the hour. For others, having seen the ashen face of a skip who's dropped a hatful on the final end to lose the match, it's something that they put on a par with having a tooth removed without anaesthetic: an experience to be avoided at all costs.

There is no disgrace either way. The beauty of bowls is that it accommodates all levels of ambition. As the haunted appearance of a bowler pressed against their will into playing skip will regularly demonstrate, those who play in that position really should want to do so. Unfortunately, in one of those profound observations often attributed to actresses in conversations with their bishops, desire and performance are two very different things. Wanting to play skip is not the same as being a good skip.

Let's stick with the nautical analogy and see if it helps. On this basis, a good skip should:

- Be an example to their crew
- Have the experience of having done their jobs – and done them well
- Be able to use the different skills of each crew member so as to overcome all manner of storms and navigational problems

---

[38] Whitman's poem was a eulogy to Abraham Lincoln, lauding him for delivering America from the Civil War and mourning his end.

- Avoid at all costs either a mutiny or a sinking, or both.

Tolerance wasn't the skip's strong suit.

Pursuing the analogy still further, do any of the better-known captains in either fact or fiction provide a role model for the aspiring skip?

Francis Drake   **Style: Abrasive, Buccaneering.**
His sterling performance against the Spanish Armada might have been his high water mark. It went to his head and he suffered many defeats thereafter. Not a very popular boy with his crews, many of whom ended up dead.
Role Model? Only for skips happy for their reputation to be based on one decent match.

Captain Ahab   **Style: Obsessive, Self-Centred**
Having lost a previous match (and his leg) against the whale Moby Dick, Ahab's single-minded pursuit of revenge ultimately costs him the rest of his body.
Role Model? Only for those with a death wish.

Captain Hook   **Style: Paranoid, Incompetent**
Frightened of a crocodile and beaten in his only serious match by Peter Pan and a motley collection of juniors.
Role Model? Definitely not. Performances could become a pantomime.

Edward Smith   **Style: Unfortunate, Resolute**
Captain of the *Titanic* who went down with his ship.
Role Model? Not unless a one-match catastrophe is the aim – albeit with musical accompaniment.

Captain Bligh **Style: Ineffective, Misunderstood**
After failing to quell a mutinous element of the crew of his ship, the *Bounty*, Bligh and a few loyal members were cast adrift in a lifeboat. This, it's not commonly known, Bligh managed to skip over 3,500 miles to safety.
Role Model? Only for those willing to lose big matches and settle for a consolation prize.

Lord Nelson **Style: Proud, Inspirational**
Both a masterful and unconventional tactician, Horatio Nelson achieved his most famous victory in the Battle of Trafalgar. His famous rallying signal, *"England expects that every man will do his duty"* would surely have included his mistress, Lady Hamilton, if she'd been on board. He was shot by a sniper and died three hours later.
Role Model? Definitely - although losing one eye, having a bit on the side and not surviving your greatest triumph would be taking it too far.

Whether or not an aspiring skip can draw inspiration from these naval counterparts, one thing should be borne in mind: none of them took part in the actual fighting. They were at the head of a team. The mathematics is simple.

- Skip playing well but Lead, Two and Three playing poorly because Skip is giving them a hard time – efficiency 25%

- Skip having an off-day but Lead, Two and Three playing their socks off to help out somebody they respect – efficiency 75%
- Harmonious combination of the best bits of the above – efficiency 100%

The committee's proposal, for rank-and-file bowlers to follow naval precedent and acknowledge their skips, was quietly shelved after the competition to find an agreed form of salute produced an overwhelming winner.

Fours Play

Bowls is a sociable game.

Other sports make the same claim, of course. Rugby is famed for its post-match sociability, with both teams coming together to wreck whatever bar they descend upon. Not so during the game, however. The speed at which things move means that – apart from the occasional grabbing of an opponent warmly by the throat – little socialising is possible. [39]

This is where bowls scores heavily. The slower pace of the game means that there's ample opportunity for players to have a chat not only after, but during the contest. On a carpet, or a green in the Southern Hemisphere, it's perfectly possible to swap life stories, with photographs, whilst waiting for a bowl to come to a halt.

This is possibly why the flagship format for bowls matches has traditionally been that of Fours rather than Singles, Pairs or Triples. With each of the players – Lead, Two, Three and Skip – delivering just a couple of bowls each, ample time is available for gossip and drink.

The social aspect aside, however, a format in which each player only delivers two bowls leaves little scope for trial and error. Foul things up, and it places more pressure on your teammates. All the more important, then, for a fours team to have a harmonious combination of talents and temperaments.

In the previous essay, skips and potential skips were given a collection of sea captains to measure themselves against. We're now going to do the same for a fours team – except that the collection of alternatives is reduced to

---

[39] Some may differ, pointing to rugby's scrummage as the epitome of sociability. Others will argue that if sociability means pressing one's cheek firmly against a quite different cheek in broad daylight then they'll give it a miss, thank you very much..

They were impressive in the fours, but had to scratch in the eights.

one. For, as bowler-fans of the original *Star Trek* series – now officially known as *Star Trek: The Original Series* - will tell anybody who doesn't see them coming, the bridge of the *USS Star Ship Enterprise* provides role models that can't be beaten.

(In what follows, only the basic details are provided for those readers whose TV education is incomplete. They are advised to fill the woeful gaps in their knowledge by watching the original 1966-69 series – and only the original series - as soon as possible. Warning: do not be satisfied with dross such as *The Animated Series* or *The Next Generation*; that would be like drinking a dodgy year's Prosecco instead of vintage Champagne. So ...)

LEAD: Spock (Leonard Nimoy)

Leads have unique responsibilities, as defined in the *Rules and Laws for the Sport*:

40.3 The lead of the team to play first in an end must:
40.3.1 place the mat as described in law 6.1.1; and
40.3.2 deliver the jack and make sure that it is centred before delivering the first bowl of the end.

Spock, part-Vulcan and part-human, had logic coming out of his (pointed) ears. He would not have joined in the verbal sparring which sometimes occurs between Skip and Lead about to where the jack should be delivered ...

LEAD: Where do you want it?
SKIP: Where you like.
LEAD You decide.
SKIP: Anywhere you can stick a bowl on top of it.

Logician that he was, Spock would have seen that for Lead to accept this argument is pure folly: no excuse will then be acceptable for their failing to draw bang on the jack.
No, he would have merely quoted Rule 40.1.1 ...

> *40.1.1. The skip will have sole charge of the team and all players in the team must follow the skip's instructions*

... and waited.

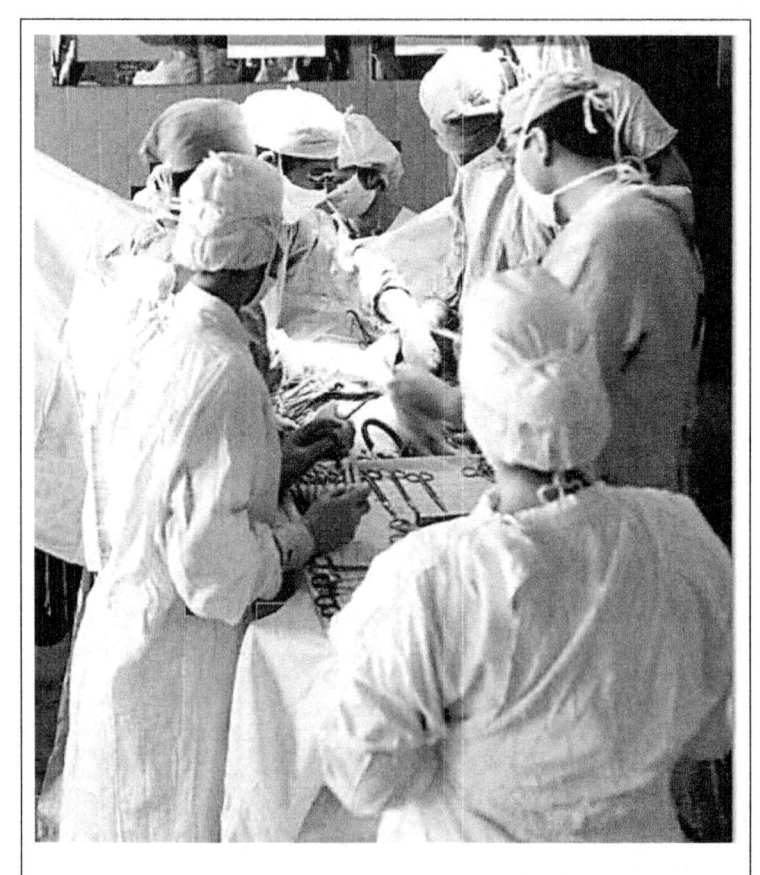

After continually being criticised for delivering the jack to where it wasn't wanted, Lead lost all patience and decided to give Skip something to really complain about.

TWO: Dr Leonard "Bones" McCoy (DeForrest Kelley)

As chief medical officer on the *USS Enterprise*, McCoy is a perfect role model for the all too often overlooked and under-appreciated Two. In particular,

- Twos are expected to cure the ills caused by a failing Lead
- They're also expected to recognise when, in spite of Lead's moaning and groaning, there's nothing much wrong with their condition and instead inject two useful supplements of their own

McCoy and Spock were known to bicker, another useful parallel – but only if it's to do with who's playing better.

Finally, the ship's doctor was not a fan of the "beam me up" process used to convey crew members to and from the planets they'd landed on. The benefits of not having to queue at passport control, he worried, were outweighed by the long-term effects of regularly having their bodies atomised then reconstituted.

Twos will take the opposite view. Usually given the job of gathering together sixteen bowls with a 'pusher' – a sort of wheeled cow-catcher – at the finish of an end and heaving them back to the new mat position, most Twos would give their eye teeth for a hi-tech "beam them back" system.

THREE: Lieutenant Nyota Uhura (Nichelle Nichols) [40]

Uhura was the star-ship's translator and communications officer, one of whose specialisms was cryptography: the bewildering science of developing and cracking codes.

---

[40] At the risk of being accused of all manner of '-isms' it has to be said that if every bowler – female and male – had legs like Uhura's then playing in shorts would have been allowed years ago.

As the member of a four charged with interpreting skip-speak, what better role model could any Three have?

In addition, opposing Threes have to communicate – and negotiate – with each other. It's they who decide the result of an end, agreeing which side has won it and how many shots they've scored. To help with this decision-making Threes can, as the rule books says:

40.2.1 ... measure any and all disputed shots.

This is not always straightforward, especially when both Threes are having a bad day with their lumbago. It's then, with the all the bowls delivered in to a very tight head, that you're most likely to witness bowls' version of the *pas-de-deux*.

Both Threes will circle back and forth, analysing each other as much as the bowls, each knowing that their counterpart is equally reluctant to get on their knees and measure in case they're unable to get up again.

This is where the communications skills of a Uhura are indispensable:

THREE: Just the one?
OPPO: Er ... looks like it.
THREE: Sure? Do you want a measure?
OPPO: (*Wincing at the thought*) No, no. Just the one.
THREE: (*Waiting until OPPO has made the fatal mistake of kicking the bowls in before calling out*) One up!
OPPO: Up? I thought you meant one to us!
THREE: Oh, no. Sorry, I thought you realised. That's why I offered you a measure. Shame. Too late now, You've kicked the head in ...

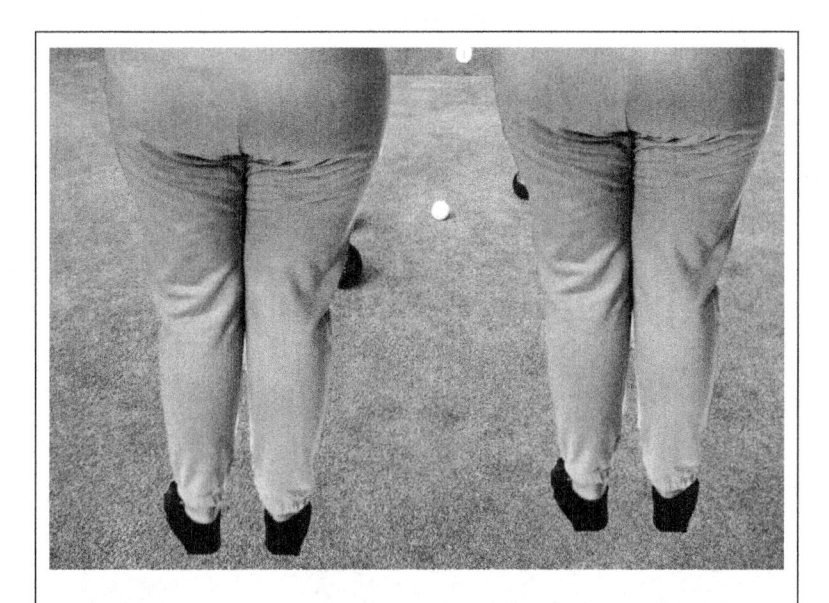

Even the most experienced skips will sometimes find that they can't see the woods for the Threes.

Skip: Captain James T. Kirk (William Shatner)

You have to admire a character, even a fictitious one, for attaining a top job in spite of having the middle name of Tiberius. Kirk's qualities as a leader trumped all. Even the one blot on his copybook, accepting the mission to "boldly go where no man has gone before" without asking whether a woman might have beaten him to it, was forgotten by the manner in which he led his crew.

Kirk talked to them. All of them. He asked their advice – yes, even of Lead and Two. Then, having listened, he acted. Skips take note.

All analogies fail at some point and this one, bowlers and *Star Trek* afficionados might point out, could be claimed to founder on the episode in which Captain Kirk and Lieutenant Uhura have a little smooch. Too far, surely!

And yet ... what was the request of the mortally wounded Horatio Nelson, our previous skip role model, to the captain of the ship he was aboard, Thomas Hardy? No word-mincing is possible: "Kiss me, Hardy," is what he said.

The implication seems to be clear. Effective fours will be those in which the skip respects the opinions of all its members and, in particular, gets on well (not necessarily *that* well!) with their Three.

"Remind us, Skip. What was it you said about our blithering incompetence after our last game - correction, your last game?"

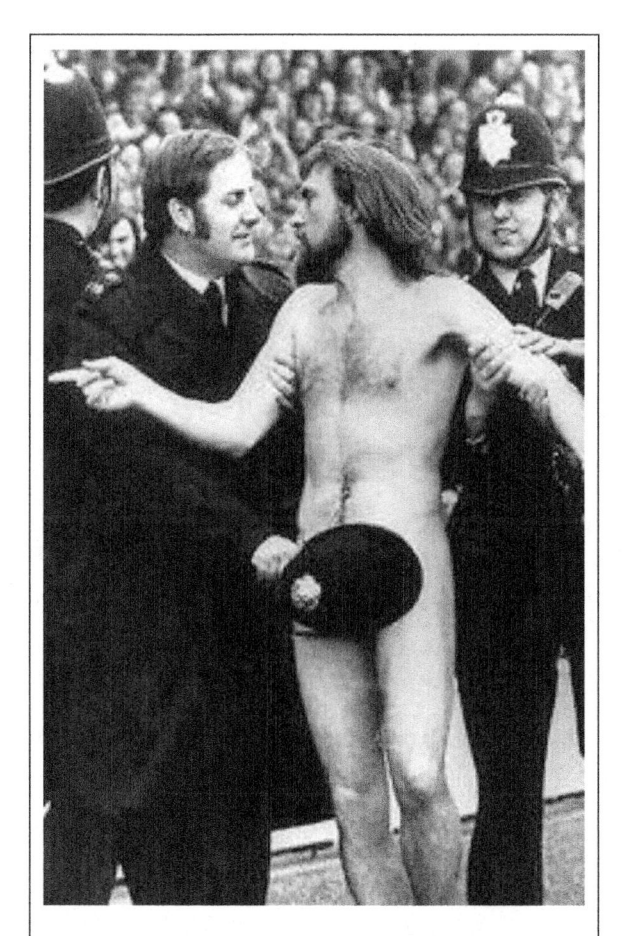

**PC Bailey was clearly *au fait*
with the standard bowls strategy
of keeping the kitty hidden**

BOWLSPEAK

SINGLES

Format in which normally hard-to-please skips become extraordinarily tolerant of their lead's performance.

PAIRS

Occasionally described as the 'organ grinder and monkey' format, although it's rarely clear as to who is turning the handle and who is peeling the banana.

TRIPLES

Bowls' version of the *ménage à trois*, the emotional ramifications of which are way beyond the scope of this book.

Skip-Speak

If the English language was subject to judicial processes, it would forever be in court on charges of petty pilfering. We've already mentioned that the words 'nuance' and 'etiquette' were snaffled from French. Now it's Greek that's on the receiving end.

'Euphemism' is the word, and it's one that all skips and would-be skips can study with profit. It's a nod to Eupheme, the Greek spirit of praise, her own name being derived from 'eu' (good) and 'pheme' (speech). In short, then, a euphemism is a mild or indirect reference to something a lot cruder, possibly offensive. There are two forms.

The first is a euphemism that everybody *knows* is a euphemism. The classic example here is the euphemism for 'sexual intercourse'. [41] We say that a couple are 'sleeping together' when everybody understands perfectly well that what they're actually doing is completely the opposite.

(They may well sleep together afterwards, of course, or have a quick snooze before 'sleeping together' again. Sleeping together *during*, however, is a really bad sign – except in the case of octogenarian bowlers with a big game in the morning, in which case it's understandable and probably recommended).

The second type of euphemism is almost the opposite of the first. It is a mild term that is used with the aim of disguising what's really going on. For example, poor wretches destined for sessions on the rack in the Tower of London might have been told that their GP had referred them for some stretching exercises. Nobles booked

---

[41] Which is itself, of course, a euphemism for a far earthier term of Anglo-Saxon origin.

for a date with Madame Guillotine during the French Revolution would have been less alarmed about what awaited them if it had been dressed up as 'helping with research into some cutting-edge technology'.

It's this second type of euphemism that skips should work on adding to their repertoire. The reason for this is that it helps resolve a permanent tension that good skips realise is part and parcel of the role, namely that:

- ✓ Maintaining a harmonious atmosphere within their team is essential - a harmony that could be destroyed if they let rip about what they really think about a shot that's just turned a two-up position into a four-down.
- ✗ If they don't say *something*, they'll explode.

It's here that euphemism earns its corn. It enables skips who have studied the black arts of this subject to yell things that can achieve the impossible: maintaining team harmony even as they simultaneously lower their own blood pressure to a safe level. What's more, they can do it before the bowl is delivered, while it's on its way and – especially – once it's stopped. Really talented skips can even manage to fit in one at each of the three stages.

The following list is merely representative. Readers could no doubt extend it by a good few pages. (Note that many would be prefixed by a mealy-mouthed formula of words such as "How about ..." or "Do you want to ...")

Before

- To Lead: "Bring the mat up"
  ("You might not be so short that way")
- To Lead: "Short / long jack"
  ("You've got nowhere near a long / short jack")

- "Try a forehand / backhand"
  (It can't be any worse than your backhand / forehand)
- "Ignore that bowl"
  ("It's on your line, so the chances of you hitting it are minimal)

Some skips find it awfully difficult not to react when one of their team fails to produce the shot they've called for.

- When the opposition have a jack-high bowl: "You can hit jack or bowl"
  ("That's halved your chances of cocking it up")
- When the opposition are holding loads of shots: "Have a go at them!"
  ("You'd never draw shot in a million years")
- After a surprisingly good previous shot: "Same again!"
  ("Famous last words")

During

- "Good start"
  ("You're raising my hopes here, but ...")
- "All on your weight"
  ("... No, you're not going to get here ...")
- "Might get lucky"
  ("... Not without a couple of wicks and a chance bounce off a wormcast")

After

- "That was the weight / line"
  ("Totally hopeless line / weight")
- "Could be useful there"
  ("If the laws of physics are suspended and the jack manages to leap backwards over a couple of bowls)
- "Could have nuisance value"
  ("It's in everybody's way – especially mine")
- "That's the best back"
  ("Miles away, but at least it's not in the ditch")

Eventually, of course, it will be Skip's turn to bowl. This is where experience really shows. It's easy to spot. As they stride towards the mat, they will insert ear plugs or turn off their hearing aids if wearing them.

That way they don't hear exactly the same set of euphemisms being directed at them.

**"I don't have a judgemental bone in my body,"
Skip managed to say without laughing.**

BOWLSPEAK

RINK (1)

Narrow strip of the green on which individual matches are played. The regulations state that it must be between 4.3 metres and 5.8 metres wide.

Related phrases: not wide enough

RINK (2)

Traditional term for a bowls Four. Why this should be so is not known. Scholars have suggested that it might be a concatenation of two words commonly heard bellowed by skips: "Rubbish!" and "Think!".

Back To The Future

As we've already seen, every bowling surface will have its little quirks. A lawn will have bumps here, a hollow or two there; a carpet, indoors or out, could have a loose stitch bang on your line to the jack. Well, here comes more bad news: they perform at different speeds, too.

The figures for the 'speed' of a green are slightly bewildering at first, because they're counter-intuitive. The winner of the 100 metres in the Olympics – that is, the quickest runner – is the athlete recording the lowest time to cover the distance.

Bowling greens are the complete opposite: the fastest greens have the highest times and the slowest greens the lowest. This is because the figure is based on how long it takes from the bowl being released to the moment when it gasps to a halt. Thus:

10 – 11 seconds   *Slow.* A typical timing for a UK green in early April, when it's very useful to have a rocket launcher handy.

13 – 17 seconds   *Medium.* Generally thought to be an ideal speed. Outdoors in the UK at the height of summer or a well-paced carpet. Bowls need a bit of oomph to get them going, but will then run on beautifully.

18 – 20 seconds   *Fast/Lightning.* Breathe too heavily and your bowl's in the ditch. Greens with speeds such as this are far more common on badly-worn carpets ... or in the southern hemisphere, particularly Australia and New Zealand.

As a helpful comparison:

About 23 seconds	Curling rink – which is composed of ice, of course. [42]

It goes without saying that green speeds affect the velocity of the bowl. What is not always fully appreciated, however, is the impact they have on a particular brand of bowler: the **Chaser**.

For a Chaser, it's not enough to deliver their bowl then watch the thing run its course. Chasers like to chase it up the green, encouraging it – if they've got enough breath – to perform this or that manoeuvre. [43]

(For some reason, skips seem particularly prone to such behaviour. Perhaps rushing up the rink to join their teammates is simply down to feelings of loneliness due to the time they spend apart. It would be interesting to hold a study on how many skips still take their teddy to bed with them.)

The speed of the green is important for a Chaser. This is because the rules of the game state that possession of the rink passes to the opposition the moment the bowl stops. In other words, the Chaser must reach the head at the same time, or even before, their bowl does. Try that on a 10-11 second green.

---

[42] That our Antipodean friends should play on greens with speeds not far short of ice is bewildering but understandable. If you're used to spending Christmas Day on the beach and cooking the turkey on a BBQ it's bound to affect your way of thinking.

[43] Bowls being inanimate objects, this is a complete waste of time. You might as well shout at your kettle to boil more quickly. Give it a couple of years, though. An Alexa-enabled bowl which will turn on command is the obvious next step in Amazon's global take-over.

Every habitual Chaser knows the importance of a getting a good start.

On a medium, and – especially – on a fast green, though, it's quite possible. If they're capable, all bowlers should try it at least once. It's a most peculiar sensation ...

- You deliver your bowl – hopefully on line
- Off you go, in hot pursuit
- As your bowl reaches the shoulder you're close behind it. You put in a bit of a burst as it begins to slow up. Suddenly you're overtaking it ...
- And are up at the head, waiting, as your bowl trundles to a halt.

It's the closest thing to travelling into the future currently available. There you are, watching the result of an action you performed in the past.

Perhaps that's why Chasers chase.

Bowls clubs often have a 'no running on the green' rule. It could be argued that, with a good few of its members needing to have a sit down after running a tap, the rule is unnecessary. Chasers, though, would see it as an argument in favour of faster greens or more carpets.

A lightning-quick green such as those found Down Under, for example, would enable a Chaser to reach the head without falling foul of the greens committee. They could get there with not much more than a gentle stroll. Moreover, their ranks could be swollen by those for whom a successful chase on a heavy green would be out of the question. The liveliness of the game could be enhanced immeasurably.

And, for the shrewd, reasonably nimble, but not-very-good bowler it could be a valuable addition to their tactical portfolio.

Instead of following the herd and only chasing after their good deliveries, such bowlers would craftily save their energy for the truly awful ones.

They would then race up the rink to arrive ages before their bowl grinds to a halt in some distant corner. By the time this happens, they'd have been amongst the players at the head for so long that, with luck, nobody would be able to remember who'd delivered it.

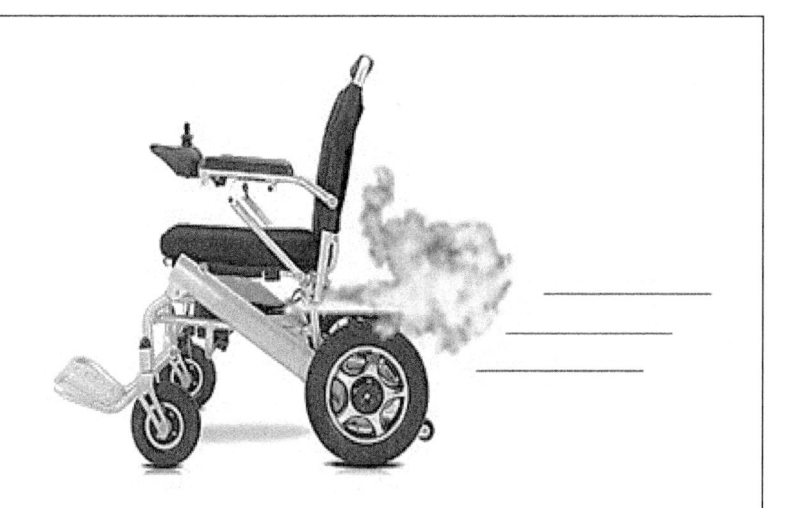

The optional attachment guaranteed that a wheelchair bowler/Chaser would reach the head before their bowl came to a halt.
Only in the small print was it mentioned that there might sometimes be occasions when they would arrive before their bowl had even started.

BOWLSPEAK

NARROW

Adjective used to describe a side of the rink which only requires the bowler to take a small amount of green to find the jack.

SWINGER (1)

Adjective used to describe a side of the rink which requires the bowler to take a large amount of green to find the jack.

SWINGER (2)

Adjective used to describe a bowler for whom the game is not their only source of entertainment.

Offices of State

For many bowlers, the least bewildering thing about the game is that of how their club functions. Psychologists would find this unsurprising. They would point out that it's impossible to be bewildered by a thought that never crosses your mind. Time to change all that. Readers who would prefer to maintain their innocence may care just to look at the pictures in this chapter.

Bowls clubs – like countries – don't run themselves. They have to be governed. For a country, this will either be through democratically-elected representatives or by a dictator supported by a heavy mob. It's sometimes difficult to distinguish between the two. For the most part, bowls clubs follow the first model with just the occasional drift across to the second.

Typically this governing body will be known as "The Management Committee" (it may operate under a different name, and/or be called a different name by club members). Elected at an Annual General Meeting, this committee will be populated by officers of various stripes: team captains, safety officer, social secretary, bar manager etc. The committees of different clubs may well have different compositions. There will be a core trio of officers, however, that are always going to be present. In the same way that governments will always have equivalents to a Prime Minister, a Chancellor of the Exchequer and a Home Secretary, the three great offices of state for a bowls club are President, Treasurer and Secretary.

(Again, different clubs could well use different names for these indispensable positions, but close observation will distinguish between them. The biggest clues are that "Presidents" are supposed to run things, "Treasurers" think they run things and "Secretaries" do run things).

The President, Treasurer and Secretary demonstrate the secret of their harmonious working relationship.

PRESIDENT

Presidential appointments invariably work in one of two ways:

   a) The President serves a one year term of office, with their Vice-President assuming the role the following year, or

   b) The President serves until such time as they either find somebody else who's prepared to do the job, they leave, or they find themselves as the guest of honour at the local crematorium.

Whichever it may be, the role of the President is crucial. To the outside world, he or she is the face of the club.

If there's an official function, it is the President who will turn up to represent the club. Should the club be visited by a VIP – the mayor, for a council-owned green for example – it will be the President who does the necessary schmoozing. And, of course, when playing a friendly match against another club, it is always our-President and their-President who run the show. Being both personable and presentable, then, are key qualities.

So, too, is a gift for public speaking – for, in these official appearances, Presidents are often called upon to

The committee had the uneasy feeling that the President was going to open their monthly meeting with rather more than, "Thank you for coming".

'say a few words'. It's times like these that sort the wheat from the chaff.

A run-of-the-mill President will oblige by providing words aplenty. Those who really understand what the role requires will know instinctively that the important part of the request is 'few'.

TREASURER

A club's treasurer has but one function: to guard the club's money as carefully – if not more carefully – than they do their own.

It's a position of considerable responsibility. We look in a later essay at bowls club economics. Suffice it to say at this stage that it's the treasurer who, like a kind of financial PE instructor, has to work late into the night counting club monies whilst muttering, "in, out, in, out, out, out, in ..."

Come the light of day, though, they know full well that what they've done will be seriously scrutinised. Even the chirpiest on-green Smiler can turn into a snarling rottweiler if the club accounts are revealed to be out by a bob or two.

It's not always appreciated how wide-ranging are the matters which are dumped onto the harried treasurer's plate. There's a lot more to the job than making sure that annual membership fees are paid promptly.

Insurance, for example. If a blasphemous screech following a wrong bias is promptly answered by a bolt of lightning which causes the clubhouse to be burnt down, who pays? [44] Ask the treasurer.

A misdirected and furious firing shot leaps from the rink, whizzes out through the gate and does a very nasty

---

[44] Act of God in this case, so no insurance pay out. Hopefully, though, the point is made.

Rather than suffer the indignity of having their pockets searched, most members ensured that the treasurer had their fees well before the due date.

mischief to a chihuahua being taken for its daily constitutional. Who pays for the funeral? Ask the treasurer.

All in all, then, it's really unfair that treasurers often find themselves the butt of financial ribaldry. For them to arrive in an expensive make of car is to positively invite wisecracks which link its purchase to the recent increase in membership fees. Exotic holiday plans get the same treatment, as if only a week spent self-catering in a ploughed field would deflect the inevitable barbs about running away with the club's funds.

Readers tempted to join in with this treasurer-baiting really should desist – unless, of course, their treasurer has indeed run away with the club's funds, in which case it's not unreasonable.

SECRETARY

If a bowls club's president is its face and the treasurer its financial brain, the club secretary is its somewhat less glamorous digestive system. Less glamorous, yes, but utterly essential. For whilst many an unattractive numbskull can live to a ripe old age (heavyweight boxers and professional footballers are prime examples), no living organism can last long without a digestive system.

The secretary's role, then, is to consume the many and varied items which constitute the everyday sustenance of a typical bowls club. Letters, emails, bills, final demands, competition details, requests to join the club, demands to leave the club, schedules for meetings, meetings themselves and the minutes thereof, complaints from the club's neighbours about excessive noise or bad parking – all are swallowed by the secretary.

S/he then has the task of extracting whatever goodness they might contain and sending it onwards. Much of the time it will go to the club's vital organs – President and Treasurer of course, but also to other important body parts such as team captains. Sometimes the nourishment will even have to be delivered to the fingers, toes and other extremities (let's not push this analogy too far) of the full club membership list.

What remains is disposed of, privately and discreetly, in a manner known only to the secretary – which is just as it should be.

All this happens without fuss or fanfare. It happens daily. It happens during the winter months, when many an outdoor club goes into hibernation. It's no surprise, then, that the better the club secretary, the more they're taken for granted – until, that is, something goes wrong. A hiccup over an incorrect date in a club circular. The acid reflux of a typo in an important letter. It's then that the single error gets a reaction whereas the countless non-errors have passed unnoticed.

Readers are asked to remember this the next time they wake up with indigestion and head for the bathroom to dig out the Milk of Magnesia. Treat your secretaries as kindly as your bowels. You'd be in a right mess without them.

The secretary's office was cramped but functional.

BOWLSPEAK

END

Individual segment of a bowls match, their usual duration being either 21 or 18 ends.

<u>Related phrases</u>: bitter end, the end is nigh, the end justifies the means, will this bloody game never end ... and many more.

TRIAL ENDS

Two practice ends played before a match begins for real – and the ends become a trial.

Looking In The Mirror

As an example of the President, Treasurer and Secretary triumvirate in action, one needs to look no further than what may well be a new bowler's first taste of competitive action: a 'Friendly'.

The wheels will have begun to turn some months before. A letter arrives, to be digested by the secretary. A club from some distant part of the country have a tour planned. They are looking for games. [45] If interested, could the secretary please reply with proposed dates and costings.

A quick check is made of the fixtures calendar, and a clutch of possible dates suggested ... and then it's over to the treasurer. Calculator in hand s/he will retire to a darkened room to emerge, sometime later, eyes glittering. It has all the makings of a big payday. Green fees for all the playing tourists; a small profit on a post-match meal not only for the players but also for the non-playing members of the party; and a seriously large profit on bar takings pre-match, during-match and – especially - post-match.

A formal response is drafted by the President, fingers crossed that the potential tourists don't get a better offer. They don't. The fixture is confirmed, high-fives shared all round, and the date ringed in red on the club calendar.

All this has happened behind the scenes. The first that members learn about the forthcoming engagement is

---

[45] Unfortunately, there is rarely any indication of whether 'game' means a competitive match or a soft touch. It depends on the nature of the tour. If it's a bowls tour lubricated by a few drinks then competition is what the visitors will be after. If it's a drinking tour punctuated by a bit of bowling for those capable of doing it without falling over, then softness with no loud shouting will be the order of the day.

when the club fixtures booklet is published. Eventually a sheet appears on a notice board seeking the names of those who want to play. Our new member takes a deep breath, puts their name down – and finds, a week or so beforehand, that they've been selected. [46]

The day arrives. The tourists draw up in their coach. The luggage compartments are opened. If they reveal more bowls bags than beer crates then a serious game is afoot. Both teams eventually congregate around the green. Their respective Presidents voice a brief welcome (occasionally, and worryingly, mentioning that they'll have more to say later) then read out their teams and rink numbers. Players head for the nominated destinations. And play begins.

It's at this point that our new bowler's pre-match nerves will begin to dissipate. Even the keenest-fought friendlies are pretty much stress-free zones. The overall result is something of an irrelevance. Such tension as exists will be down to any developing possibility of ending the game as 'best rink' – or, at the other end of the scale, trying to dodge the stigma of being named and shamed as 'worst rink'.

But, like closing and opening doors, as nervousness departs our new bowler could well find it replaced by another emotion: surprise. Having, until now, lived a sheltered existence of coaching sessions and roll-ups, this initial encounter with bowlers from another club is about to teach a lesson well-known to those who've been hospitalised with some strange lurgy – namely that,

---

[46] 'Selection' is only the right word to use in cases where the numbers saying they're available to play exceeds the number of players actually required. When this isn't the case it usually results in a phone call from the President or an aide-de-camp saying, "You're selected. Are you available?" *Conscription* is the term the military use.

Not being able to join in with the bowls tourist's pre-match preparations was the worst part about being their coach driver.

believing they're unique, they pitch up in Ward 5B only to find the place full of fellow-sufferers.

So our novice, accustomed to playing the odd game marvelling at Mabel's original delivery style in which she leaves the mat at right angles, discovers that her action isn't a one-off at all. It's also employed by another bowler, living 160 miles away – except that this one is male, with a stomach the size of a zeppelin and four-lettered words tattooed on the fingers of each hand.

Likewise the club's oldest member who, before playing every shot, pauses statue-like on the mat for so long that you begin to wonder if the club defibrillator needs to be rushed out. Astonishingly, he too has a counterpart: a sprite of a girl who, irritatingly, justifies the delay by plonking her every bowl bang on the jack.

But the worst may be yet to come. From an adjacent rink comes a howl of pain. A visiting bowler has given their shot far too much green. They're waving an arm in circles, desperately encouraging the bowl to do what was intended even though it's giving every indication of not listening. When finally it comes to a halt somewhere in the back of beyond, there's a deep sigh and a shake of the head before they trudge forlornly back to the mat.

That's when it happens. The new bowler feels a nudge in their ribs and the voice of a teammate chortles, "Just like you!"

In a very tight contest, the host club's champion beat the touring club's by 21 frowns to 19.

In Praise of Ham Salads

The visiting President got to her feet. This was the first friendly of her Presidency and she was going to make her point. And, after handing out the awards for her club's 'best rink', she made it.

"It is now customary to give consolation prizes to what has traditionally been called the 'worst rink'. I do not like this term. 'Worst' is horribly negative and I have vowed, during my term as President, always to seek the positives. The term 'worst rink' will never cross my lips."

"So -" She picks up a scorecard and gazes around the room. "Our most pathetic rink was ..."

The game is over. The players leave the green and, together with visiting non-players and guests, congregate in the clubhouse. Our new bowler is about to experience a few time-honoured traditions ...

GENEROSITY

Players from the host club are expected to buy drinks for their opposite numbers in the match just completed. This is a lottery. It could be that zeppelin-stomach will go for a small lemonade, but if he's been on the receiving end of a pasting then drowning his sorrows with something large and expensive is more likely. The host player simply has to smile thinly and cough up. [47]

---

[47] If the pasting has been in the other direction, the smile could be thinner to the point of vanishing.

RINK TABLES

Wedding planners could take lessons from bowls clubs when it comes to seating arrangements. Simply put, players who have just shared a rink now share a meal table.

What is easy to plan, however, is not necessarily easy to live with. Hosts and tourists who have got on well and enjoyed a closely-fought match are fine. Those who've been on the end of a thumping have more trouble. It'll be they who will look for small-talk on any subject other than bowls and spend more time than usual in munching their ham salad.

Yes, the much-derided ham salad (or ham-less salad for vegetarians) is most likely to provide the bill of fare. And why not? It's tasty, provides scope for a load of accompaniments, and can be plated up well in advance (although a fortnight would be pushing it a bit).

"Now that was what I call a ham salad!"

GUEST TABLES

A corollary of having rink tables is that guests – camp followers of the touring club and non-playing spouses / partners / friends of the host players – will necessarily be seated at separate 'guest' tables. That such a high-risk strategy seems never to have been questioned is quite bewildering.

Consider the composition of a typical guest table. From the tourists there are bound to be a good sprinkling of Shakers – possibly, if the host club is located in an attractive part of the country, even an unreconstructed Scoffer for whom sitting through a game of bowls is an acceptable price to pay for a few day's holiday. And, literally rubbing shoulders with them (clubhouses tend not to be palatial), will be Shakers belonging to a few of the host players.

This is madness. It's akin to taking every con-artist and embezzler and lumping them together in the same prison wing so that they can spend their period of incarceration sharing successful methodologies and best practice.

No wonder that bowlers – whose home Shakers have hitherto been persuaded that five games a week is not unreasonable – suddenly find themselves being told that every other day is quite sufficient; or Shakers who haven't previously questioned the line that an alcohol-lubricated post-match inquiry is part and parcel of the game now – the wool having been pulled from their eyes by a granite-jawed touring Scoffer – start imposing curfews.

SPEECHES (including 'the joke')

With the inevitability of night following even the sunniest of days, there will come the point in the proceedings at which both the home and visiting Presidents get to their feet and say their few words.

For the most part these words tend to be fairly harmless. References to the weather and the enjoyable game. Thanks to all concerned (especially those who prepared the meal; to forget this is the sin of sins). Awarding of prizes for 'best rinks' and consolations for those at the other end of the scale. [48]

So far, so good. Presidents who want to earn the undying gratitude of their audience will sit down now. Sadly, few do. They feel impelled to tell a joke.

Curiously, some will begin by saying that they're no good at telling jokes before proving so in spades. Others will say they found this one in a joke book in their dentist's waiting room, subtly making the point that it's not their fault if it isn't funny.

Either way, bowlers being polite people, they'll get a laugh. However, this is a very tricky judgement call for the audience. Weak laughter will offend, and nobody wants that. But guffaws and eye-mopping could be even worse; they could encourage the speaker to tell another joke. Then, not to be left out, the rival President feels the need to tell a second. Before you know it, the tourist's resident comedian is weighing in and you've got a full scale non-comedy club on your hands that's very difficult to stop.

THE RAFFLE

One – perhaps the only – thing that can be said in favour of the ubiquitous raffle is that it's a good way of putting a halt to a joke-fest. Clubs able to provide a visual interruption by means of a brightly flashing electronic raffle

---

[48] These (including – and sometimes especially – the consolation prizes) are highly likely to be in the form of memorabilia emblazoned with the President's name and the year. It's a crafty way of ensuring their period in high office remains unforgettable, even if their performance wasn't.

number generator are at an advantage here. If it plays a few bars of *Colonel Bogey* when turned on, even better. Hosts and tourists will have known a raffle was coming at some stage. Tickets would have been prominently displayed on all the tables, with receptacles for money. Any profit is a bonus, though, since most of the income will have been pre-spent on decent prizes to supplement those donated by host members.

It's these decent prizes which always go first. Winning ticket holders will head for the bottles like wasps to a jam sandwich. Next will be chocolate boxes, quickly followed by other tasty edibles. Once these have gone, the tipping point is reached. Detectable to the experienced raffler's ear by an increase in background chatter, we're down to the prizes that nobody gives a stuff about winning.

Until now there's been a generally altruistic hope on the part of the hosts that the tourists will pick up their fair share of the prizes. No longer. Now, with only the endlessly re-donated lavender toiletry pack left, such impartiality goes out of the window. This is a prize a tourist *must* win. It won't stop the blessed thing turning up in yet another raffle, but at least it'll be one held a hundred-odd miles away.

FAREWELLS

And so the day comes to an end. The tourists are escorted from the premises and back to their coach, hopefully with one of them already mulling over how soon they can get shot of this bloody lavender toiletry pack they've just been landed with. Our new bowler joins in with the general goodbyes and heads innocently back to the clubhouse to pick up their stuff and head off home.

No such luck. The clubhouse looks like a bomb – or, at the very least, a touring party – has hit it. Volunteers are being called for to help clear up. If the newbie can escape with wiping a couple of tables and stacking some chairs they should be very grateful. At some clubs they'd be met at the door by the President wearing a funereal smile and holding a pair of rubber gloves.

"Club tradition, I'm afraid. Worst rink has to do the clearing up, and you were one of them. Still, look on the bright side. Not everybody is taking home one of my presidential ballpoints and a packet of Love Hearts."

Had she been too generous when the bowls club asked for raffle prize donations? For goodness' sake, that lavender toiletry pack had cost her 3½d !

Your Very Good Health

Only one thing is worse for a bowler than having to argue with a Scoffer, and that's having to argue with a Scoffer who's got a gym membership. "Bowls? Exercise?" will scoff the Scoffer. "You're having a laugh. I burn more calories climbing on my Peloton bike!"

The fact that the said Scoffer might then spend the next forty-five minutes on a gentle trundle over some nice flat virtual reality country roads whilst working through the play-list on their iPod is neither here nor there. The barb has struck home. The poor bowler slinks away, chastened and feeling inadequate.

Time, then, to marshal an aggressive response to such a slanderous jibe. For those who prefer purely verbal rejoinders, the argument should be along the following lines: [49]

"What? You're talking through your padded lycra, my friend. You clearly have no idea how much skeletal flexibility, muscular generation of forceful impetus and anaerobic movement is involved in the playing of our noble sport ..."

That may be all that's necessary to send the Scoffer scuttling for cover. If not, the next threat might: "Let me give you the numbers, my friend ..."

If that doesn't work, the next bit almost certainly will – the numbers themselves. Here they come. They're based on a standard triples match of eighteen ends plus two trial ends; it is left as an exercise for the reader to come up with the figures for alternative formats. (Those allergic to maths should jump to the end-of-chapter summary).

---

[49] Expletives can be added at will, but the fewer the better. The bowler is aiming for the moral high ground here, and a barrage of effing and blinding tends to take the edge off things.

SKELETAL FLEXIBILITY (aka Bending Down)

The essential point here is that in order to bend down and deliver a bowl, it firstly has to be picked up. That's two bending downs, [50] each bending down being equivalent to the PE instructor's staple exercise of touching your toes. So ...
- 18 ends plus 2 trial ends = 20 ends played
- 3 bowls delivered each end plus 2 each on the trial ends = 18*3+2*2 = 58 bowls picked up and then delivered
- Thus, during the match, a bowler <u>touches their toes</u> 58 * 2 = <u>116 times</u>. [51]

MUSCULAR GENERATION OF FORCEFUL IMPETUS (aka Bowling)

There are two sets of figures here, because we're not just talking about pumping melamine but also of forcing these weights (bowls) into travelling a distance.

Weights first:
- The lightest lawn bowl available, a size 0000, tips the scales at just over 1 Kg. At the heavier end, a size 5H weighs nearly 1.6 Kg. If we take the average of 1.3 Kg, then ...
- Every bowler <u>lifts</u> 58 x 1.3 Kg = <u>75.4 Kg</u> during a triples match. That's equivalent to 3 sacks of potatoes (probably *Maris Piper* although it's said that *King Edward's* are making a comeback).

---

[50] A previously unmentioned health benefit of not being a Chucker and launching them from an upright position. Not only is bowling smoothly good for the green, it's good for the player.

[51] Leads get bonus points here, because they also have to pick up and deliver the jack. No wonder Leads always look in such rude good health – apart from the worry lines across their brows.

**Touching their toes wasn't a problem;
it was straightening up again.**

Now forceful impetus.

Having lifted the bowl, it then has to be delivered to the jack. This takes effort. ⁵²

Let us assume that we're playing a full-length (35 metres) jack on a green timed at 14 seconds – a typical UK summer speed. (Oh, yes. And you never send up a short one.)

---

⁵² Antipodean and carpet bowlers are at a disadvantage here. When you only have to breathe on your bowl to get it to the other end, it's difficult to claim you're putting in a lot of effort. Once again, if the information isn't volunteered then it can't be questioned. Think like a politician, in other words.

- The standard jack length for timing a green is 27 metres. It'll take longer for a bowl to travel 35 metres: 35/27*14 = 18.14 seconds.
- We now need to work out how fast the bowl has to be started off at in order for it to come to a rest after 35 metres – that is, its initial velocity. (Ignore line. Many bowlers do, so it doesn't invalidate the calculation.)
- The magic formula is ...
  initial velocity = (2 * distance travelled / time taken) – final velocity
  = (2*35/18.14) – 0
  = 3.85 metres / second
- Concentrate now, it's about to get tricky. Setting a 1.3 Kg bowl off at a speed of 3.85 metres / second is to give the thing kinetic energy. Another magic formula is involved:
  Kinetic Energy = 0.5 * weight of bowl * initial velocity ^ 2
  = 0.5 x 1.3 x 3.85^2
  = 9.63 Joules
- A simple bit. The effort expended by the bowler in transferring this energy to the bowl is exactly the same number, but with different units: 9.63 Newtons.
- So the total effort expended to deliver 58 bowls during a triples match is: 58 x 9.63 Newtons
  = 558.54 Newtons.
- So what? Here's what. The average standing-still adult exerts a force on the ground beneath their feet of about 608 Newtons. Thus – and here's the Scoffer-mangling bit you've been waiting for:

- During a triples match a bowler <u>expends almost enough energy to send their own body weight up to a full-length jack.</u>

This is not something done by your gym-membership Scoffer. Ask one how far they throw the barbell they're so proud of lifting and see the look of bewilderment cross their face.

The free "*Develop Your Bowls Muscles in a Month*" plan he'd downloaded had some innovative exercises but the cost of train tickets was prohibitive

ANAEROBIC MOVEMENT (aka Walking)

After the complications of the previous two components, this one is a walk in the park.

$$\text{Distance walked} = 20 \text{ ends} \times 35 \text{ metres}$$
$$= 700 \text{ metres } (0.43 \text{ miles})$$

Add a few extra metres for helping to gather the bowls together at the conclusion of an end, wandering to the bar and loo, retrieving wrong biases from an adjacent rink etc. and <u>the bowler walks about half a mile</u>.

Summary

For those who've jumped here, or those who've nodded off on the way, here's all you need to remember for your Scoffer counter-attack:

During the average triples match a bowler will touch their toes nearly 120 times, walk about half a mile, and expend almost enough energy to propel their own body weight the length of the green.

No wonder we always drive home from the club.

BEFORE **AFTER**

The *Frowners Anonymous* sessions had certainly done Gordon a power of good ... but they'd worked almost too well on the bloke who'd tagged along with him.

BOWLSPEAK

TIED END

End in which the two closest bowls are judged to be equidistant from the jack – sometimes after exceptionally careful measurement, sometimes because neither of the Threes fancies getting their knees damp.

DEAD END (1)

End in which the jack, either deliberately or accidentally, has been knocked beyond the side boundaries of the rink.

DEAD END (2)

Repeated attempts by a bowler to find a line to the jack – either because it doesn't exist or because the bowler isn't good enough.

DEAD END (3)

Creeping sensation felt by members of the management committee when their monthly meeting yet again passes the two hour mark.

Money, Money, Money

There is a push nowadays to introduce personal finance into the school curriculum. Teach the little herberts that everything has its price, the argument goes, and they will be less likely to max out their credit cards before they leave primary school. This is commendable. Of more importance, however, is the fact that by studying the principles of balanced budgets the young stars of tomorrow won't get quite such a shock when they eventually discover the costs of playing bowls.

To be fair, they're not huge. Compared to motor racing, flying and ocean racing, they're miniscule. But they exist, and it's as well for a new bowler to be aware of them. Who knows, should they fail to aspire to the heights as players they might nevertheless achieve high office as a club treasurer.

(In what follows, the operation of the ever-present bowls club bar is ignored. This is not because it's unimportant – quite the opposite – but because it's often run as an independent entity, with its own set of accounts. Two provisos are common. Firstly, that the bar must make a profit. And, secondly, that the majority or all of this profit should be transferred to the coffers of the club. This arrangement needs to be made very clear to club members for, once it has been, many will be prepared to go the extra mile or ten in their enthusiasm to swell club funds)

Expenditure

In Charles Dickens' novel *David Copperfield*, the character Wilkins Micawber famously proclaims (in pre-decimal coinage):

> *"Annual income twenty pounds, annual expenditure nineteen nineteen and six, result*

happiness. Annual income twenty pounds, annual expenditure twenty pounds nought and six, result misery"

Micawber is a clerk, but he could equally well have been the treasurer of a bowls club. Getting in more than you pay out is essential. So, before looking at the costs involved in playing, the reader is invited to reflect on the typical outgoings of their club:

Given his dedication to maximising bar profits, members were happy to put up with the inevitably wayward bowling.

- *Greenkeeping* (salary, equipment, grass nutrients and pesticides ...)
- *Clubhouse* (maintenance, insurance, furniture, decorating ...)
- *Services* (heating, lighting, water, rates ...)
- *Affiliation Fees* (national body, county and district associations ...)
- *Equipment* (mats, pushers, scoreboards, scorecards ...)

It may not have been the swankiest of clubhouses, but at least it didn't have to be painted every year.

This list can be expanded or contracted but never done away with. Whatever the annual bill comes to, it has to be covered. There are only two ways of doing this:

1. Extract money from bowlers as the *quid pro quo* for being able to play their game
2. Extract money from non-bowlers: that is, achieve the seemingly impossible task of getting people to part with their money even though they'll never set foot on the green.

Let's look at each, and consider the dark arts involved.

BOWLERS

Membership Fee – a club's staple source of funding. Confirmed by vote at the AGM (so that nobody can argue that they didn't see it coming), all club members pay it. Various categories of membership, and membership fee, usually exist. Typically:

- *Full* (allowed to play)

- *Partial* (can play, but is not registered to represent the club in competitions: aka 'a roll-upper')

- *Junior* (assumed to be in poverty, so allowed to play at a reduced rate)

- *Associate* (not allowed to play, but for around 10% of a full membership fee can sit on the side lines shaking/scoffing and take part in all of the club's social activities). [53]

---

[53] Some clubs have a *Life Vice-President* category of membership. Conferred on distinguished members as a reward for many years of service to the club, LVPs don't have to pay a bean. For this reason, if recipients are still allowed to be active players, they tend to be limited in number so as to restrict the loss of membership income. An attractive alternative is for LVP status only to be conferred on members who have retired from the game ... or be offered as an incentive to do so.

Little did piggy-wiggy realise, but just as soon as his tummy-wummy held enough for a junior membership fee he was going to find himself splattered into lots of piecey-wieceys.

Green Fees – a levy on visiting bowlers in return for their being allowed to sample the delights of the club's green. Every player will be able to provide instances of visiting greens on which, if any justice existed in the world, money would have been transferred in the opposite direction and the bowler paid to play on it. That is by the by; whether the green is good, bad or we'd-have-done-better-to-play-in-the-car-park, a green fee will have to be handed over.

The exception is for club league matches in which a return fixture has been or will be played. Then it's a simpler matter for the home players to hand over the green fee and get a free ride when they visit their opponents' place. That at least enables bowlers visiting a car-park green to comfort themselves with the thought that they've had their no-money's worth.

Social Events – open to bowlers and non-bowlers alike. The stated objective with these is to offer something a little different to bowls. (Different is the operative word here; the offering can't possibly be superior).

Darts competitions and whist drives provide outlets for members' competitive instincts, whilst talks, singers, strippers – male and/or female – can give the associate members something for their money. Usually such events are not going to make the club lots of additional revenue, but if there isn't a spike in bar takings then questions need to be asked.

NON-BOWLERS

Extracting money from non-bowlers is an order of magnitude more difficult. If the benefit to coughing up isn't being allowed to play the game, then another benefit has to be provided in its place. So ...

Hire of Clubhouse – within reason, and if a damp-squib insurance policy doesn't forbid it on the grounds of 'elf and safety, hiring out the clubhouse can be a source of useful income.

The price has to be carefully set, though. Lower than a 5* hotel's function room isn't difficult, but making it too cheap might suggest to the potential hirer that what's on offer is an empty space with a few tables and chairs. This is to be avoided – especially if what's on offer is an empty space with a few tables and chairs.

Timing is also important, particularly during the playing season. Members will take umbrage if they find they can't get from green to loo in a hurry because the premises have been hired out to a horde of screaming youngsters celebrating a birthday. (Unless, of course, the screaming youngsters are also junior members, in which case they'll be quite used to being harangued by apoplectic oldies with bladder problems.)

Grants & Awards

Many altruistic bodies offer grants for various purposes. So, on occasion, do local councils and/or councillors. Access to any of these slush funds, however, will always require a case to be made. [54]

Fortunately, bowls clubs are in a strong position here. "Health" and "fitness" are a couple of buzz-words which will make ears prick up, especially when linked to the equally attention-grabbing terms, "young people" and "elderly".

Presidents, treasurers and secretaries who can get their heads together and explain in a compelling way the health and fitness benefits of our sport for both young and old can make a big difference to a bowls club's financial position.

Advertising & Sponsorship

Persuading businesses to advertise themselves through the club, or to sponsor some aspect of the club's activities is to tackle two sides of the same coin. The aim of both is to get the advertiser's / sponsor's name in front of those who might be interested in whatever product or service

---

[54] Where councillors are concerned, the case needs to be rather more persuasive than "cough up or we won't vote for you."

Top Tip: grant applications to provide bursaries for young and old who can't afford a membership fee will be immeasurably enhanced by including photographs which tug at the heart-strings

they have to offer. Strange as it may seem, then, the first thing a bowls club needs to identify is what areas of blank space they might have available.

For example, on:

- The club's web-site
- Fences surrounding the green
- Clubhouse walls – interior and exterior
- Scorecards
- Club Shirts

The next step is to convince the potential advertiser-cum-sponsor that if, for a financial consideration to be determined, they were to put their name in that space then it would undoubtedly be followed by a flood of interested people wanting to know more about what they've got to offer.

This is not easy. Inevitably, the potential advertiser / sponsor will ask the obvious 'bang for buck' questions: a flood – or a trickle? And how interested? It's the reason that the likes of retirement villages, solicitors specialising in wills and the avoidance of inheritance tax and yes, funeral directors, are the most fruitful avenues to explore. For them, just one or two clients will more than justify the cost of their involvement. [55]

For a bowls club this is a virtuously vicious circle, however. It generates valuable income, but perpetuates the impression that bowls is a game for those who, if not exactly having one foot in the grave, are plodding steadily in that direction.

The solution surely lies in clubs' own hands. Truly inter-generational clubs will attract inter-generational advertisers and sponsors. On the sordid 'bang-for-buck' principle, a local college could be persuaded of the benefit of putting its name in front of junior bowlers who could one day be the sources of tuition fees; or the local

---

[55] Nor, to be horribly blunt, keep them waiting all that long before they see a return on their investment.

estate agent made to see that they could recoup their sponsorship money from a single first-time buyer or down-sizer.

Let's look forward to the days when the *Little Terrors Nursery School* is as likely to advertise its services with a bowls club as the *'Here Today, Gone Tomorrow'* *Funeral Plan Company.*

Cradle to grave bowls club sponsorships. That's what we need.

Shirt sponsorship by the South Hampshire Institute for Technical Excellence, though lucrative, definitely had its down side

Booked Up

"Would you be prepared to have sex on the television?"

The potential Love Island contestant took a deep breath. This was it. Her reply was crucial. Get it right and exposure – in every way – would follow, with fame and fortune close behind.

So far the interview had gone well. The interviewers had nodded with satisfaction at her body piercings. Not too few, but not so many that she looked to be suffering from woodworm. And her tattoos had been exceptionally well received, especially the Chinese lettering on her forearm.

"What does it mean?" they'd asked.

"Make love, not war," she'd lied. Well, it would have meant that if the tattooist hadn't got his copy sheet back to front. Now it actually read, *"Is this the bus to Beijing?"* It had been a tricky moment, but she'd got away with it.

This was it, then. The big one. The chief producer was impatiently drumming her fingers on the table. She asked the question again.

"Well? Would you be prepared to have sex on the television?"

"Yeah, I suppose. I mean, a bed's comfier like, but ..."

It used to be the case that there were those who would do anything to get their faces (and, nowadays, other body parts) on television and those who weren't interested. No longer. We're all on, whether we like it or not.

The explosion of CCTV systems means that even a quick trip to the Co-op will have you popping up on more screens than Gary Lineker, but without the inflated salary. Road monitors, parking cameras, shop surveillance systems – we're the unpaid stars of them all.

Camera-free zones are becoming as rare as check-out operatives in a supermarket. No wonder mask-wearing became surprisingly popular during the pandemic.

For the most part, however, this infection has yet to reach the humble bowls club. CCTV is an avoidable expense. Cameras outside, recording the comings and goings at the clubhouse, have little value. They'd have to be accompanied by high-power lighting to get a decent shot of any nocturnal visitors – who, besides, would probably be even more covered up than a bowler in the rain. And even if the local cat burglar was snapped, what would be done with the CCTV footage? Only if the club is covered by some hefty insurance would it be worth contacting the CID. [56]

After all, it's not as if too many clubs have a lot to steal. Apart from bar stock – which, at a vibrant club, is often managed on a 'just in time' basis anyway – there isn't that much to attract a crook. A few of the club's more garish trophies perhaps, those that even in their moments of euphoria the winners were sufficiently clear-minded to realise wouldn't quite go with their home décor.

And that's it, really. Organised Crime is more about stealing and exporting top-of-the-range Ferraris than the sort of stuff found in most bowls clubhouses. It's hard to believe that somewhere in the darker reaches of the criminal underworld there's a Mr Big growling out of the corner of his mouth to an underling, "Get the word out. I've got a sheikh willing to pay big money for half a dozen formica-topped tables, brown, no ring marks."

No, there's only one reason that would make it worth having a CCTV camera in a clubhouse: it would be really, really intriguing to have it permanently trained on the books-for-sale shelf.

---

[56] Counselling and Indifference Department.

During their de-clutter of the 'books for sale' shelf, the committee decided that 23 copies of *Bowls for the Bewildered* was too many; 23 too many.

Every club has one. Members donate books they've finished with, or never even started. Other members pay a small price and take them away – until they too bring them back to this literary merry-go-round. [57]

Members brought up on a diet of reality TV programmes could find viewing the CCTV footage irresistible. Who donates what? Who buys what? Does their skip's favourite genre have any relationship to their

---

[57] A merry-go-round, the books' authors will point out bitterly, from which they derive no financial benefit whatsoever.

performance or demeanour on the green? Treasurers, take note. It could be a real money-spinner, a club's very own reality subscription channel.

Think about it. Who wouldn't enjoy seeing ...

- One of the club's less tolerant skips donating what looks like a new and unopened copy of *How To Win Friends and Influence People* in exchange for a copy of *The Godfather*?
- A renowned Frowner picking out *Les Misérables* and *The Grapes of Wrath* for a bit of cheerful bedtime reading
- A red-faced new bowler returning *How To Draw* after discovering that its advice on cartooning wasn't a lot of help
- The female half of a couple whose club mixed pairs match had ended in acrimonious defeat, and whose husband hadn't been seen since, popping a copy of *Agatha Raisin and the Quiche of Death* on to the shelf. Then, a little smile playing about her lips, returning for the bookmark she'd forgotten to remove from the chapter in which the recipe is revealed.
- An irritated member who'd been hoping to learn something about the crown green game paying good money for *Wuthering Heights*, only to bring it back the next day.
- One of the more conceited men's first team skips walking out with *Mr Perfect*, supposedly for his five-year old son, then being called back to receive a copy of *Where's Wally?* that the other three members of his rink had clubbed together to buy for him – the little lad, that is.

Had they known that their skip had recently donated *Crime & Punishment* to the club book stall, his triples colleagues might have been more wary of sarcastically referring to him as 'a barrel of laughs'

- The vain bowler, still refusing to bow to the inevitable and get a pair of reading glasses, dumping a weighty volume on the shelf whilst muttering darkly, "I thought the bloody title was *Lord of the Rinks.*"
- And, the highlight of the programme, the couple who'd recently celebrated their silver wedding anniversary. She, bright-eyed and bushy-tailed,

whose recent form has been sparkling. He with bags under his eyes and the haunted look of a bowler who's no longer on speaking terms with the jack. She dips into her bag and takes out a well-thumbed volume, the corners of umpteen pages turned down for easy reference. Looking this way and that, she sighs dreamily and pops a bonus ten-pound note into the money box. Finally, fondly, as if saying goodbye to an old and dear friend, she slides *Fifty Shades of Grey* back on to the shelf.

Wearing a face mask during the pandemic came as nothing new for those who'd experienced the perils of cleaning the men's changing room after they'd played in a downpour.

BOWLSPEAK

"BEST BACK!" (approvingly)

Bowl deliberately delivered closer to the ditch than any of the opposition's. The aim is to provide a safeguard in case the jack is sent into the ditch.

"BEST BACK!" (sarcastically) - 1

Bowl accidentally delivered not only miles past the jack, but even further past than any of the opposition's.

"BEST BACK!" (ultra-sarcastically) - 2

First bowl of an end, delivered by an over-enthusiastic lead.

In League With Each Other

Having successfully negotiated roll-ups and friendlies, new bowlers will be ready, in contemporary parlance, to take their game 'to the next level'. This will almost certainly mean performing in one, or more, of their club's league teams. (The implied assumption here is that with league play 'the next level' will be higher. This is by no means guaranteed).

Leagues are a central part of the local bowls scene. Variations occur everywhere, of course, but typically there will be leagues of women's teams, men's teams and mixed teams. Depending on the number of clubs in the locality, a league may have a number of divisions, with end-of-season promotions and relegations adding spice to the arrangements.

How, then, does our new bowler get selected for one of the club's teams? That depends on how seriously the club takes things. Some may go so far as to have a selection committee which meets in secret enclave before finally emerging to post team-sheets on a notice board surrounded by bowlers trembling with excitement. Others may simply pin up blank sheets asking for volunteers, with teams chosen from those willing and – hopefully – able to play.

Whichever approach is taken (and often it's a combination of the two), a common thread is another of a bowls club's unsung heroes – the team captain.

There may be worse jobs in a bowls club, but it's difficult to think of one. Clearing the clubhouse gutters of dead leaves and pigeon droppings or fumigating the clubhouse toilets the day after the bi-monthly Curry Night don't come close.

Consider the list of awesome responsibilities shouldered by a team captain ...

When it came to being selected for a mixed team, Marcus Antonius was known for hedging his bets

Select the Players

A potential lose-lose situation if ever there was one. Assuming that more bowlers are available than required, somebody is going to feel aggrieved at being left out.

Can anybody blame captains if they sneak into the clubhouse under the cover of darkness to pin up their teamsheets and thus avoid the not-so-*sotto-voce* mutterings: "Reserve? What am I, a bottle of bloody Port?"

Decide the Teams

A typical fours league team might comprise anything between two and four rinks: eight to sixteen players. Selecting those players is just the first step for a captain. If that activity is fraught with danger, arranging them into fours can be positively life-threatening. Knowing who gets on with who and who can't bear to share the same green – let alone the same rink – as who, is an essential part of the role.

Fill the Gaps

It's a fact of captaincy life that there will be occasions when the number of available players falls short of the numbers needed. Out-of-town matches seem to be particularly vulnerable, especially those against clubs with greens like corrugated roofing. Diplomatic skills that would earn a top job in the Foreign Office now have to be employed to fill the gaps. Favours are called in and the captain's phone bill takes a hit as they desperately attempt to drum up the required numbers.

Deal with Drop-Outs

All this necessarily needs to be carried out a week or more in advance. Now, as the day of the game arrives, captains who've been round the block a few times know not to relax. Another challenge is but a phone message away.

"Sorry, but I can't play tonight ..." The excuses may vary, but the problem doesn't. If the captain's fill-the-gap skills were tested before, now they have to switch into overdrive as the poor wretch dials the number of a player

Too late did the captain realise that he'd made the catastrophic blunder of putting Mrs Blenkinsop on the same rink as Mr Blenkinsop

still seriously miffed about being omitted from the team in the first place.

"I tried to give a game to somebody less <insert smarmy compliment> than you and they've gone and let me down ..."

And then, as if the above weren't enough ...

Repeat as Often as Required

League teams are just that – teams which compete in a league, the principle of which is that every team plays every other team both home and away. A league of 10 teams means 18 matches for which the captain has to go through this rigamarole every time ...

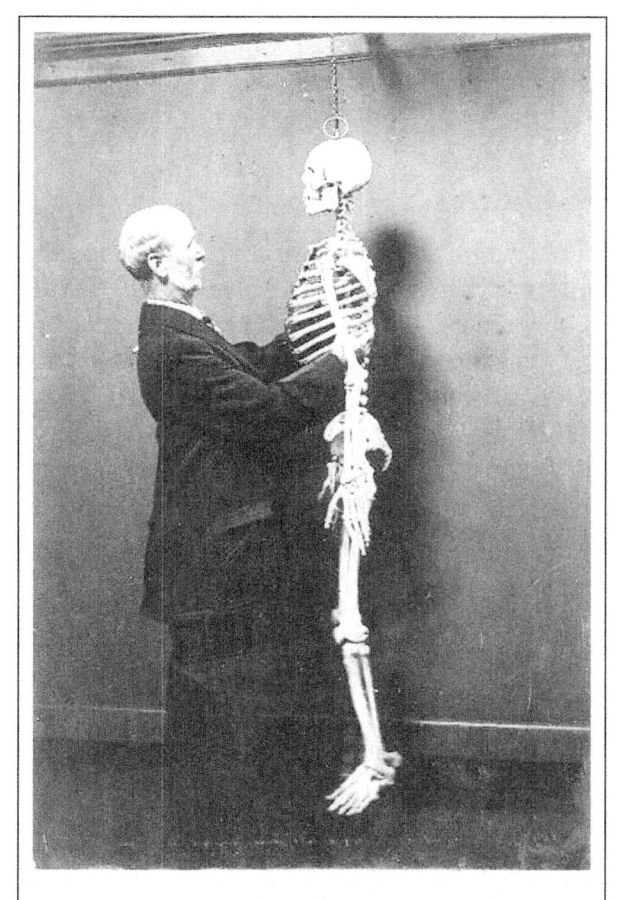

"Doctor, do you think it could be the stress of team captaincy that's making me lose weight?"

Whether by choice or expediency, the frazzled team captain has called on our new bowler's services. S/he has been selected for one of the club's league teams. It may be at home, on familiar territory; it may be away, on a strange green. What can our newbie expect to learn from the experience?

In short, a bit more about their approach to bowls – but a lot more about strategy and adding up big numbers.

All Bowls Matter

Our new bowler will experience an odd sensation on the green, one not felt when playing roll-ups or friendlies – namely, that their bowl actually *matters*. It stands a chance of making a contribution to the team's score, a score which at the end of the game will be transmitted to a league organising apparatchik seated in a dimly-lit room with a glowing spreadsheet in front of them.

Knowing that an end which finishes with our newbie's bowl(s) as part of a count – or even holding the solitary shot – adds that extra bit of pressure to get things right. It also helps to explain why long-standing league skips have so many worry lines etched across their foreheads. It's like posting to the internet that ill-advised selfie of you playing your part in the Platinum Jubilee celebrations wearing nothing but a union jack; one day the evidence may come back to haunt you.

The Worst Rink Paradox

One crucial fact that novices will come to realise about league bowls, especially if they're numerate, is that it's simultaneously possible to be both totally useless and the hero(ine) of the hour.

This is due to the generally-applied scoring system which, for bowls league matches, operates at two levels: rink points and match points.

Typically, the side that comes out ahead on any one rink will earn two points. Thus, in a four-rink fours match there will be eight points to be won. Now for the mathematical bit. Shots scored on each rink are aggregated to give an overall match score – with the team that wins the match clocking up an additional eight points.

Thus, an all-rinks win will leave the triumphant club celebrating a 16-0 victory. A more evenly-balanced match might produce a score of 12-4, derived from both teams winning on two rinks but with the match points earned by the side ahead when the shots are aggregated.

This is where the paradox can come in to play. Here's an – admittedly contrived – example.

Our new bowler is taking part in a four-rink match against their near-neighbours and fierce rivals, Carnage BC. As the proceedings draw to a conclusion, fortunes are mixed. Our newbies' club have won 20-10 on each of the other three rinks – giving them 6 rink points and putting them 60-30 ahead overall.

But our new bowlers' rink is getting obliterated. They are 0-30 down ... meaning that the overall match score is level at 60-60.

One end behind the other rinks due to having to cope with so many big numbers, our new bowler – playing as Lead – steps on the mat ... and, for the first time in the whole match, sticks one bang on the jack. And there it stays. Try as they might, the Carnage four are unable to budge it. To roars of celebration, our newbies' rink take the final end to give the team a 61-60 overall win and a points win of 14-2.

This is the paradox. Only in league bowls could a team that's just been smashed 1-31 swagger off the green to back-slaps all round.

Not only were the skips of the three-rink
ladies' team the best bowlers
in the club, they could also calculate
the current match score in a jiffy.

It's A Knock-Out

Representing one's club is a fine and noble thing to do. However, it may not take our new bowler very long to decide that representing oneself is just as noble and – on a successful day – a damn sight finer.

What this entails is entering a knock-out competition: that is, a competition in which you're in it until either you win it or, much more likely, get beaten. Bowlers who are statistically-minded have been known to equate the business to finding success in the National Lottery. The more entries they make, goes their thinking, the greater their chances of winning something. They are confusing luck with talent, of course, but there are parallels. Entering a bowls competition, like buying a lottery ticket, costs money – with the odds being overwhelmingly in favour of both sums disappearing down the plughole.

No matter. Within our new bowler's heart there beats the Olympian Spirit. S/he is still a firm believer that it's not the winning that matters, but the taking part. And where opportunities for taking part are concerned they've undoubtedly chosen the right sport. Bowls competitions are like buses in Switzerland: miss out on one and there's bound to be another you can catch in a minute.

For instance, any bowler – from international to novice – can cough up their fee and try to win, in descending order of impossibility:

- National competitions
- County competitions
- District competitions
- Club competitions

At each of these levels, there are the standard set of formats available, namely:

- Singles
- Pairs (Men's, Women's or Mixed [58])
- Triples (Men's, Women's or Mixed)
- Fours (Men's, Women's or Mixed)

Plus, as if this lot wasn't enough to occupy every daylight hour, a collection of competitions for which entries are either genetically- and/or age-restricted. The bewildered bowler can easily recognise these types of competition because they will always employ our old friend the euphemism in their title. For example:

- Family Pairs (*Squabblers' Pairs*)
- Senior Triples (*Knocking On A Bit Triples*)
- Retired Singles (*Over The Hill Singles*)

How exactly the validity of entries to such competitions is confirmed remains something of a mystery, DNA testing and birth certificate examination not yet being required. Presumably bowlers are expected to have familiarised themselves with the entry conditions and honestly believe that they satisfy them ...

---

[58] 'Mixed' means the appropriate numbers of each flavour. Thus –
- Pairs (one plus one)
- Triples (one plus two)
- Fours (two plus two)

Partners in life can often be tempted to venture as partners on the green either in a pair, or join with another pair to form a four. This is a high-risk strategy. Launching tea-cups at each other is bad enough, but swapping 3H Drakes Pride Professionals is another matter altogether. Needless to say, joining a couple as the third in a triple should always come with danger money attached.

As she admitted to the magistrate when her case came up, she really should have studied the entry requirements for the 'Golden Pairs' competition more carefully.

The deadline for entries has passed. Now, whatever the level of competition, the process is pretty much the same. Administrative wheels begin to turn. Behind a locked door sits a human punch-bag known as the Competitions Secretary. Alternately applying an ice pack and downing coffee strong enough to stop a rhino in its tracks, s/he collates the entries. This done, the draw is made. [59] It's published. Our novice(s) fall upon it with gusto, eagerly searching for their names. Aha! They're at home. And they now know who their opponents are going to be.

Our fledgling entrants are about discover how important are the qualities of guile, concentration and tactical awareness when it comes to knock-out matches. Not in the playing of them – they're just bowls games. No, it's arranging the blasted things that calls for real skill. Without it, time spent on the phone can well dwarf that spent on the green.

To be fair, competitions secretaries do their best to help. Every draw will have been accompanied by a set of dates for the different rounds. These will be in one of two forms: 'play-on' dates, or 'play-by' dates.

'Play-on' dates are great. Unfortunately, they tend only to be applied to fours and triples competitions. This is understandable and recognises that getting up to eight bowlers at the same venue on the same date is as difficult as getting a batch of candidates at a general election hustings to agree on how the country should be run – especially when at least one of them is a member of the Monster Raving Loony Party.

'Play-on' dates render negotiation unnecessary. The game is played as scheduled and, unless the visitors fail to turn up or the hosts refuse to answer the door, all the competitions secretary needs to do is await the result before updating their spreadsheet.

---

[59] This used to be done by 'senior management', often with the aid of bingo equipment. Nowadays a competition draw is far more likely to be made 'by computer'. This is understandable. Not only does it take up far less time, the computer can't argue back when it's blamed in the event of a cock-up.

Every year the Competitions Secretary left entrants in no doubt about the fate awaiting them should they fail to play their games on time.

    It's 'play-by' dates, especially for pairs competitions, that seem to cause the most problems. The draw will have designated the home players as 'challengers' and it's their duty to propose match dates to their opponents. [60]

---

[60] That the term 'challenger' conjures up images of a cuckolded husband slapping his wife's lover's face with his glove and demanding satisfaction (*in lieu* of that which his opponent has had) is not wholly inappropriate. Lessons could be learned. Clearly there would logistical difficulties in requiring a challenger to formally set matters in motion by assaulting their opponents with a damp bowls cloth, but the accepted scheduling of 'tomorrow at dawn' could solve an awful lot of problems.

And thus begins the merry-go-round ...

CHALLENGER: I'm calling to arrange our pairs game.

OPPONENT_1: What pairs game? I'm not in any pairs competitions this year.

CHALLENGER: County pairs. Yours is the number on the draw sheet.

OPPONENT_1: Oh, sod it. My partner must have put me down for it.

CHALLENGER: I've got some dates to offer you.

OPPONENT_1: You'll have to ring my partner. I'll give you the number ...

CHALLENGER: I'm ringing to arrange our pairs game.

OPPONENT_2: What pairs game?

CHALLENGER: County pairs. Your partner's given me your number.

OPPONENT_2: Oh, sod it. I wanted to get out of all this arranging lark. That's why I didn't put my number down.

CHALLENGER: I've got some dates to offer you.

OPPONENT_2: (*Sighs*) Let's have 'em, then – but I can't agree to anything.

CHALLENGER: Why not?

OPPONENT_2: Because I'll have to check 'em with my partner first ...

Eventually, after interminable to-ing, fro-ing and excuse-making, accommodation will be reached and the match completed minutes before the play-by deadline. That's OK. It's when the play-by date is breached that the poor competitions secretary really feels the heat.

Should the challenger, as the rules usually say, be chucked out and the opponent given a walkover? Not so easy, not when the challenger calls to insist that they've provided three reasonable dates as required and every one of them has been rejected due to the opponent's supposedly frequent commuting to the local hospital, having to either deliver or visit or fetch an elderly relative who's been having an embarrassing condition treated.

Expel the opponent, then? Not when the opponent is insisting that if the challenger thinks three offers of eight o'clock in the morning is being reasonable then they need their bloody head tested.

Expel them both? Tempting, too tempting – and who can blame a competitions secretary who succumbs to the temptation rather than come up with a judgement that would have had Solomon scratching his head?

None of the possible decisions are pleasant. However, they're definitely easier to make for the secretaries running national, county or even regional competitions. At least they're not likely to meet one of the offended entrants down some dark alley. Pity, then, the club competitions secretary called to referee a dispute between the daughter of the club champion and the bloke giving Presidential lifts until the drink-driving ban has run its course. Chucking out one, the other, or both, is to invite the heavens to fall in.

Ultimately, and whatever decision is made, the rule book may have to be dusted off and the nuclear passage underlined: "the competitions secretary's decision is final". And who can blame the poor secretary for making sure that final it certainly is, by tendering their resignation? Which would be a pity. For, as anybody who's tried it will tell you, the role of competitions secretary would be very rewarding were it not for the competition entrants.

Was the famous Belgian fountain a more accurate metaphor for the tribulations faced by challengers or by competitions secretaries? It all depended on which end of the water stream you had in mind.

It had been a slow period for donations in the charity shop and the 'Fantasy Wear' rail only had two items – one summer, one winter

BOWLSPEAK

SCORE (1)

Every end of a bowls match results in one side scoring as many 'shots' as they have bowls nearer to the jack than any of their opponents'. Any bowl that has contributed to this score is said to have been 'in the count'. In team play, modesty is expected of those who have contributed scoring bowls. The correct phrasing is 'one to us', not 'one to me'.

SCORE (2)

End by end, these shots are accumulated so as to give a running total for both sides – the score. A side that hasn't yet scored is said have scored zero.

SCORECARD

A private copy of the score which is maintained, usually by each of the skips, during the match. At the end of the match they should match. A skip whose team has been on the receiving end of a pasting may well hold their card aloft and ask if anybody's got a match.

SCOREBOARD

A public copy of the scorecard. Much deplored by battered teams, who would prefer to grieve in private.

Marking Time

"I want to be alone," famously said Greta Garbo's misery of a depressed ballerina character in the 1932 Oscar-winning film *Grand Hotel*, "I just want to be alone."

Had she been a bowler, she'd have been a Frowner for sure. Worryingly, she also sounds as though she'd have been a dedicated singles player. The two elements have an unfortunate habit of going together. There are fairly obvious reasons for this.

Singles involves the question of personal pride that other formats do not. Being a member of a triples or fours team, for instance, allows ...

- A dodgy performance to be overlooked if it's counter-balanced by your teammates' brilliance.
- Blame for a defeat to be transferred elsewhere, especially in the direction of the lonely bowler at the other end of the rink
- Results, good or bad, to be quickly forgotten in the post-match socialising

To play singles, however, is to face the other side of the coin:

- ✗ Dodgy performances can't be counter-balanced; you're on your own
- ✗ The same goes for the blame game; defeat is down to you alone
- ✗ For post-match socialising over a friendly pint, read post-match brooding over a bottle of scotch

But this is a specimen of coin yet to be unearthed by any archaeological dig. It's got a third face:

- ✓ Brilliant performances are down to your talent alone
- ✓ No blame, just glory. And it's yours, all yours
- ✓ The brooding scotch becomes a very well-deserved celebratory drink(s)

To play singles, then, is for the bowler to put their head above the parapet; to put their talent – or lack of it – to the test; to prove that when Rudyard Kipling wrote in his poem 'If' ...

> *If you can meet with Triumph and Disaster*
> *And treat those two imposters just the same*

that, Nobel Prize winner or not, the bloke was talking through his hat.

Curiously, this is easier the higher one aims. Lose a singles match in a national or county competition and one is given credit for trying in the first place – rather like the sympathetic treatment that Useless United from the Totally Useless League receive when they enter the FA Cup and are obliterated in the first preliminary round.

No, if you want to see Frowners by the cart-load look no further than your average bowls club's singles. There you'll see ...

- No-hopers frowning at the prospect of failing to beat an even-less-hoper
- Middle-rankers frowning as they psych themselves up to play against the bowler who, for unfathomable reasons known only to their club's blinkered and wholly incompetent selection committee, has been preferred as a second team lead all season
- Champions and potential champions frowning because, should they lose their match, the

news will be on the club grapevine within seconds [61]

And, finally,

- Those – at whatever level – who have come out as challengers on the draw sheet will be frowning because know they've now got to deal with the occupational hazard of singles play: finding a marker.

Yes, singles matches require the challenger to recruit a marker. The precise duties of this essential third party we will ignore for now. Suffice it to say that the marker does some administrative stuff and saves the two players an awful lot of walking.

The important thing to realise at this point is the dire nature of what the challenger needs to do – namely, to try and persuade a fellow bowler to spend a couple of hours on a bowling green ... *and not bowl*. Admittedly, to a very small minority this might come as a blessed relief, but to most bowlers it comes as a request from hell. Stalking a potential marker, then, requires guile and strategy.

For example, our new bowler has entered the club singles and come out as a challenger. Amazingly, the opposition has immediately accepted one of the offered dates and times. The match is set for the following Tuesday afternoon. All our novice has to do now is recruit a marker (aka victim). A potential is spotted, wandering aimlessly around the clubhouse. Our new bowler now makes the classic blunder, asking "Any chance you could mark for me next Tuesday afternoon?"

---

[61] The fact that it's a handicap singles in which the champion was giving away 18 shots and lost only to a wick from outer space makes no difference; a champion's defeat is always big news.

Direct requests such as this are doomed to failure. A glazed expression will inch into the victim's eyes. Teeth and/or dentures will be sucked. One of the old guard will feign deep thought as they consult some mental diary, whereas the younger techno-savvy types will fish out their phone and check a carefully-shielded electronic calendar instead. The end result is the same. "Sorry, I'm already <something plucked from a well-used list>"

**Of all the books in the club library,
'1001 Excuses For Not Being A Marker,
And How To Deal With Them'
was by far the most well-thumbed.**

No, this a chess game. Potential markers have to be played like the King, slowly being backed into a corner from which there's no escape ...

BOWLER:	Hi! Season going well?
VICTIM:	Not bad. Up and down.
BOWLER:	Playing much?
VICTIM:	Usual. Mixed league. District pairs. Club roll-ups.
BOWLER:	Sounds like a busy week coming up.
VICTIM:	Not too bad. Roll-ups on Monday and Friday. League on Tuesday. Pairs on Thursday.
BOWLER:	Day off on Wednesday, eh?
VICTIM:	(*Sighs*) Yeah.
BOWLER:	(*Spotting the opening*) Decorating?
VICTIM:	(*Gloomily*) If all else fails.
BOWLER:	Can you mark for me on Wednesday?

Checkmate. The victim has nowhere to go. The fact that the bowler's match was fixed for Tuesday is a minor matter. A quick phone call is all that's needed. "We'll have to play our singles match on Wednesday, I'm afraid. The marker I'd lined up has let me down and that's the only day my replacement can manage."

With time comes experience. As our new bowler slowly becomes a not-so-new and then a not-new-any-longer bowler, persuading fellow bowlers to mark for them becomes an increasingly regular occurrence. They will then realise that in the above scenario a couple of vital questions were omitted:

- "Have you entered for any singles competitions yourself?"
- "Have you been knocked out yet?"

If the answers to these are 'Yes' and 'No' respectively, then the tables will almost certainly be turned before very long. "Remember I marked for you? How about you marking for me?" is moral blackmail that takes a strong will to combat.

And, perhaps, our bowler won't want to combat it at all. Perhaps they will have started to realise that, as regards playing ability, the limit for them is likely to be a fair bit lower than the sky; more garden shed height.

Then, in the same way that football freaks with limited talent stand a better chance of running out at Wembley if they concentrate more on refereeing than playing, so the prospect of becoming a qualified bowls official might grow increasingly appealing. If that's the case, regular marking is the place to start. [62]

As mentioned previously, the role of the marker is to do some administrative stuff and save the players' legs. Expanding things a little more, this means that the marker will:

- Keep the scorecard and operate the scoreboard, ensuring that both are in synch. The trailing player rightly gets a bit upset if, with the scoreboard showing 19-20, their marker suddenly waves the scorecard and chirps, "Game over. I forgot to put one up on the last end."

---

[62] Those wanting to know the details of a marker's duties, or those looking for an inexpensive cure for their insomnia, are referred to section 42, subsections 42.1, 42.2, 42.3, 42.4, sub-subsections 42.1.1 – 42.1.2, 42.2.1 – 42.2.15, 42.3.1 – 42.3.3 and 42.4.1 – 42.4.3 and the relevant sub-sub-subsections of *Laws of the Sport of Bowls*.

- Carry out essential rules-based jobs, like making sure that after delivery the jack is within bounds and centred
- Answer questions that the players might pose during the game – and *only* those asked. There are only three possible replies to the query, "Am I holding shot?", for instance: "Yes", "No" or the equivalent of "It's a measure." A monologue along the lines of "You're holding two, maybe three and if you knock his nearest out with your last you stand a good chance of a four" is bad form.
- Measuring close bowls, but only if asked. Don't volunteer. Let the players get wet knees.

Nothing was said, but both players got the distinct impression that their marker wasn't anticipating a game needing many close measures

Oddly, the rule book only lists the DO's of marking. It's curiously silent on the – in many ways – equally important DON'Ts. So, to fill in gaps, here are a few:

- ✗ No laughing, hooting or snorting in derision, however abysmal the shot just played
- ✗ No head-shaking, no holding sides in mirth, no body language at all that can be construed as a commentary on what's happening
- ✗ No favouritism. This applies especially to any spouse/partner marking for their other half. Bias one way or the other is not on. However difficult, revenge measuring because of a spat over the breakfast marmalade has to be resisted. Maintain strict neutrality until you both get back home and hostilities can be resumed.

If this all seems a bit much, and nothing like as much fun as playing, bear in mind that – when doing the job for carefully-chosen players – marking can make a serious contribution to a bowler's all-important self-confidence.

Apart from executing a perfect draw, there's little that can give it more of a boost than leaving the green after marking and thinking, "Well, I may not be brilliant but surely hell would have to freeze over before I played as badly as that pair."

Birds Of A Feather

Many a true word is spoken in jest, it's said. The same goes for derision.

"You must be cuckoo," Shakers will say gently as their resident bowler arrives home after playing in weather that would have caused Francis Drake to think twice about putting to sea. Scoffers would use one or more additional words, applied with considerably greater emphasis: "You must be <expletive(s)> cuckoo!"

The comparison has an element of truth about it, even though the implication – that the dedicated bowler is bonkers – hopefully does not.

This is because the common European cuckoo is a migratory bird. Come the chillier weather, the little things sensibly up sticks and fly off to somewhere a lot warmer. Outdoor lawn bowlers do exactly the same thing, except that instead of a marathon flight across the Mediterranean Sea and the Sahara Desert their migration route probably involves no more than a five-minute spin in the car.

This is to simplify things slightly. It's not just temperature drops that get the lawn bowler on the move. It's also to do with the design characteristics of grass which, for reasons best known to itself, refuses to grow in the winter. To play on a green during the months when it's unable to recover from the treatment handed out by even the smoothest bowlers – let alone a dive-bombing couple of Chuckers – would be disastrous.

Come the middle of September (in the UK) then, lawn bowlers are faced with two choices: do nothing or do something.

Doing nothing may be a reasonable choice for a bowling couple with other plans – a world cruise or his 'n' hers hip replacements, for instance – but for a bowler with a Scoffer to deal with it's pure folly. To spend a whole winter away from bowls is to positively invite the pointed suggestion that to give up the whole of the following summer wouldn't be much different, would it?

No, no, continuity is the key. At all costs, the lawn bowler must continue to bowl. And that inevitably means joining the Great Migration and becoming a carpet bowler for the winter months. The choice is simply one of destination: outdoor club or indoor club?

As we've seen already, outdoor clubs with a carpet instead of grass are able to stay open all year round. As many compete against lawn clubs during the summer months it's not simply a case of business as usual when autumn leaves begin to fall. Even though in practice they're just ploughing on regardless, carpet clubs will still divide the calendar into 'summer' and 'winter' seasons. This is helpful for the migrant, since a 'winter membership only' is often available at a bargain price.

The advisability of taking this migratory route depends very much on how the bowler views fresh air. If it's an essential part of their game then an outdoor carpet club is the right destination.

Not only will the delights of wind and rain continue unabated, they'll be enhanced by the excitement of sub-zero temperatures and the risk of hypothermia. Come the Spring our migrants cannot fail to return to their lawn clubs glowing with weather-beaten good health – a small price to pay for losing a couple of toes to frostbite.

Less hardy bowlers will opt for migration to the more tropical climes of an indoor club. Arriving *en masse,* they will quickly renew acquaintances with the indoors-all-year-rounders and play will begin.

The two groups will be very easy to distinguish. The permanent indoor bowlers, their sun-denied appearances giving them the air of a vampire with a faulty body clock, will be those plonking their bowls right on the jack.

For the outdoor Boxing Day roll-up, warmth took precedence over style.

The migrants from outdoor lawn clubs, although tanned or rusty depending on what sort of summer it's been, will be identifiable by sound alone. Used to putting in a bit of effort, they'll be the bowlers producing all the thumping noises as their bowls clatter into the ditch without slowing down.

> "Here come the outdoor bowlers. Same old story, every year. Temperature drops a couple of degrees and the wimps are on their way."

It takes a little time, but the migrant soon gets the hang of things again. Before long they're playing as many short bowls as ever. Even the frustrations of playing on a surface that requires the precision of brain surgery are forgotten when they hear the sound of hailstones pounding on the roof and cast their minds back to the middle of July and the match that was abandoned due to a monsoon.

It's a different game, indoors, but it's the same game too. Roll-ups, leagues and competitions; lines to find and weights to calculate; wicks which can do their business from even further out; wrong biases which can threaten a game being played two rinks away.

The highs and the lows also. Stunning or got-out-of-jail victories; crushing, slower-motion defeats; Frowners and Smilers; all there.

And then – just as you're getting the hang of it – Spring arrives and it's time to fly again.

BOWLSPEAK

"NOT UP!"

Crude way of telling a player that their bowl has wilted before reaching its intended target.

<u>Alternative phrases</u>: many, all x-rated.

"FIRE!"

Command to deliver a bowl at high speed, the aim being to scatter the bowls that others have sweated blood to get close to the jack.

"YARD ON"

Request for a player to deliver their bowl so as to – notionally – stop a yard behind the jack. The intention is often, but not always, to dislodge an opponent's bowl. One of the least-known benefits of Brexit. Remaining in the EU would have meant that bowlers would have had to change the cry to, "Nought point nine one four metres on."

And The Winners Were ...

Competitions, by definition, have winners – and winners are normally recognised either by the award of trophies or money; ideally, both. [63]

Bowls clubs follow this pattern; they may well have created it. Winners' trophies, either specially purchased or donated, will exist in abundance. Some will be stylish. Some will look like the protype for a suspension bridge. Many will have a figurine of a bowler on top, delivering their bowl with an action that most club members – possibly even the winner – couldn't emulate in a month of Sundays. All have to be presented. This basic fact of competition life thus begs the question: how to do it?

After all, winning a knock-out competition normally requires success in a few matches at least. (Prospective national champions are looking at a dozen or thereabouts). To greet the winners as they walk off the green with their trophy in a Sainsbury's carrier bag – albeit a top of the range, use it time and again carrier bag - just doesn't seem right somehow. Triumphs such as these demand an element of the ceremonial. Which is where Presentation Evenings come in.

The idea is laudable: present winners with their trophies in front of an audience of their peers. (The fact that more than one of those peers could still be smarting at having been knocked out by the winner's outrageous fluke on the extra end must always be ignored). This ceremony can be as a separate section of another gathering – such as the AGM – or, if you're looking for a

---

[63] School sports days are the exceptions here, too many having adopted the 'prize for taking part' approach. Winners should rightly feel upset about this, and ask if they'll be given A grades in their examinations should they do no more than turn up and snooze quietly.

decent turnout, at a gathering that is anything but the AGM.

Presentation Evenings fit the bill nicely. Turned into a social event, evenings such as these are well suited to clubs with members spanning the spectrum of age ranges. The youngsters don't have to stay up too late, and neither do the oldies. And all can see, in the prizes being distributed, the club's dynamism. For the club which is truly dynamic won't simply reward competition winners.

Clubs with active junior sections will encourage dedication and commitment with a *Most Improved Junior Bowler* award. (An award best voted for by the juniors themselves to stave off criticism from parents of not-the-most-improved juniors). There'll be awards for those who contribute behind the scenes. *Coach of the Year*, for example. And definitely no booby prizes. There should be no part to play for the likes of *The Wrong Bias Trophy* or *Ditch-Finder of the Year Award*.

An alternative to a Social Gathering-cum-Presentation Evening is to go way up-market and hold a Presentation Dinner & Dance. There are arguments for and against.

Against is that clubs tend not to foot the entire bill, so prize winners wanting to receive their deserved acclaim will have to pay for the privilege. Another is that dances necessitate the provision of music: almost certainly a disco plus DJ. The upshot of this is that it can lead to the youngest and oldest club members giving the event a miss: the youngest because they wouldn't know any of the music and the eldest because no composer has yet come up with a decent disco anthem for geriatric and walking frame.

On the plus side, however, is the argument that everybody gets something out of the event, prize-winner or not.

It had been a frustrating season and, as she said in her acceptance speech, "being awarded the soddin' *Top Contributor to the Swear Box Trophy* has just about taken the bleedin' biscuit!"

There's the meal of course, but also the chance to dress up. Bowlers whose idea of elegance on the green is wearing matching socks invariably surprise one and all by scrubbing up remarkably well. Evening dresses sparkle. Dinner suits, accompanied by only slightly less sparkly bow ties, appear to fit.

Sometimes it's only when the couple you vaguely recognise from somewhere get on to the dance floor that you pin them down. Ah yes, regulars at the Friday roll-up, looking like a million dollars but spoiling things by proving that the tendency for their limbs to move in random directions isn't limited to their performances on the bowling green.

All enjoyable stuff, but essentially sideshows to the main purpose of the event. Throughout the evening glances have invariably strayed towards a table groaning under its glittering collection of trophies – many of them retrieved from lofts and given their first buffing since being put up there almost exactly a year ago. Time for them to be redistributed.

As the winners are identified and applauded, faces try not to show bewilderment at how the hell they did it. Memories of painful defeats worm their way back to the surface, only softened if the defeat was inflicted by the eventual winner. Then it's possible to nod approvingly before turning to one's neighbour and murmuring, "Well played. Had to beat me to win that, y'know."

Trophies will be carried back to dinner tables to be admired by fellow bowlers and even by Shakers and the odd grudging Scoffer. And then it's over. Music will begin to pound again, drinks will flow and the trophies will find themselves cheek by jowl with bottles and glasses.

All too soon it's time for the final skirmishes of the evening to be played out ... to decide who takes the trophy home.

Their pleasure at winning the Farmers' Bowls Association's Mixed Pairs title had quickly evaporated when they were handed the trophy.

For singles trophies it's clearly straightforward. The winner is lumbered. Pairs, triples and fours are far more difficult. Usually the groupings have been drawn out of the hat and the winners have demonstrated the double luck necessary to do well in such competitions: draw useless opposition and brilliant partners. [64]

Perhaps our new bowler had this sort of luck. In the triples competition s/he ended up with a friendly skip and a supportive Two. Now, as the three of them gaze at a triples shield the size of a small surfboard, Skip gives the newbie a friendly smile.

"You played really well. I think you should have the trophy."

Two nods supportively, "Couldn't agree more, Skip."

And so, after a maximum of forty-eight hours spent as the centre of attention on the dining room table, our new bowler lets down the loft ladder and carries up what s/he hopes will be the first trophy of many.

---

[64] The feigned joy shown by a *Strictly Come Dancing* professional when partnered by the has-been politician with flat feet has no place in a bowls club. Treasurers looking for a boost to the takings of their club's swear-box should post themselves within earshot of the noticeboard when the draws are pinned up.

Keeping Your Head Down

Bowls clubhouses rarely need to have their interior walls painted, for the simple reason that you can rarely see the walls for noticeboards.

Noticeboards to a bowler are like watering holes to an elephant. They provide sustenance, of course, but also serve as a place to meet other elephants and have a good old gossip about elephantine things. The difference is that whilst elephants tend to frequent just the one watering hole, bowlers are spoilt for choice.

Team sheets for forthcoming games need to have the bowler's desire to play marked on them, then revisited to confirm that the captain has seen sense and picked the right team. Competition draws need to be assessed when first posted, then repeatedly checked – either to discover next opponents during a successful run or in vindictive hope that the lucky so-and-so who beat them has received their deserved come-uppance in the next round.

There will be notices about the state of the green, the progress of club teams, copies of league tables, details of forthcoming barbecues, darts matches, karaoke nights, district information sheets, county information sheets, national information sheets, letters from visiting dignitaries thanking the club for their warm welcome, letters of complaint from neighbours following the clubhouse alarm malfunction, and more. Any new notice – especially if a large 'read this' pointy finger is attached to it – will quickly gather a crowd. Except for one ...

Efficient secretaries usually try to pin it up a month or so before the end of the season. Like many similar notices around the walls this, too, is looking for members to add their names. And yet, unlike requests for players or attendees at the end-of-season fish-and-chip jamboree, this one doesn't attract an eager, pen-wielding crowd.

On the contrary, long-standing members will give it no more than a furtive glance before shuffling quickly past, eyes now downcast as if checking their shoes for signs of wear and tear. They've seen all too many previous incarnations. The Annual General Meeting is on the horizon and this is the notice, headed "Election of Club Officers", appealing for nominations. As usual, it is disconcertingly and threateningly blank.

The exceptions to the furtive-glancers are those for whom the notice is fresh and interesting: namely, our new bowlers. They will stop and gaze at it in awe.

At its length, for a start. So many positions to be filled. Not just the big guns, such as President, Treasurer and Secretary, but the lesser lights. Team Captains by the bucketful, Secretaries for Membership, Fixtures, Internal and External Competitions, Safety Officer, Bar Manager, Bar Volunteers ... even a couple of honest Auditors to confirm that the Treasurer and Bar Manager have done their sums correctly.

More than anything, newbies will notice the acres of white space where names of the nominated should be. A fleeting shaft of altruism will pierce their hearts. Should they offer themselves? No, leave it for another year or two – at least until they can regularly get a bowl to stop within hailing distance of the jack.

Days pass. Slowly, faithful stalwarts begin to add their names to show that they're prepared – if not exactly willing – to continue in office. When this happens, the speed with which Proposer and Seconder signatures appear alongside the nominees is in stark contrast with what's gone before.

Old hands watch all this unfold until the last day of the season. Then, when they think nobody is watching, they give the list a final once-over. Damn. There are still some positions to be filled.

The conclusion is clear. Seats in the back row at the AGM are going to be at a premium. [65]

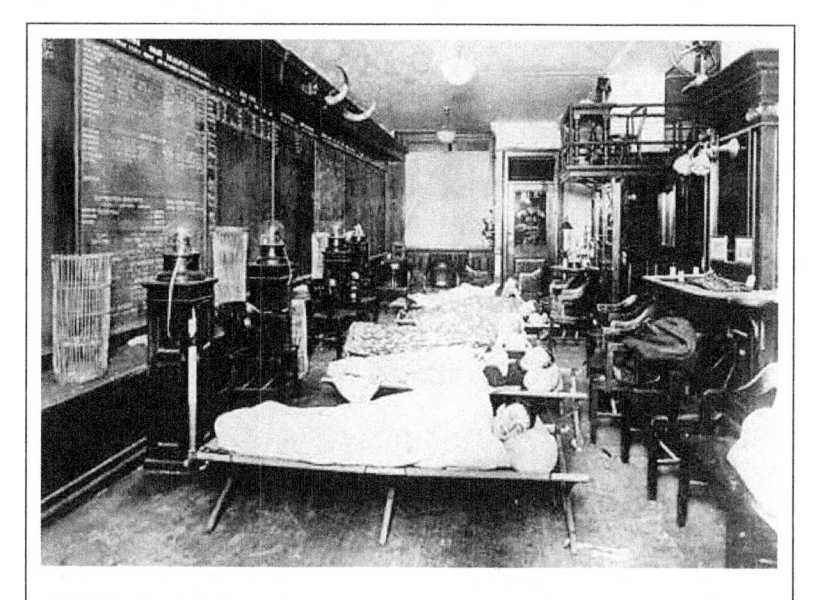

With limited numbers of back row seats available at the AGM, desperate measures were called for

A bowls club's Annual General Meeting is like watching England play football: long periods of tedium punctuated by the odd moment of hilarity or terror.

---

[65] Newcomers may wonder why it's not sufficient simply to send a heartfelt 'apology for absence', blotched with a couple of tear stains for added effect. This is to miss the point. Real bowlers pride themselves on showing moral fibre both on and off the green. For them it is a matter of principle to attend the AGM and show that, when push comes to shove, they can always be relied upon to not stand up and not be counted.

(We refer here, of course, to England's so-called "Lions" men's team and not the "Lionesses", recently crowned European Women's Football champions. Rarely has the dictum, 'the female of the species is more deadly than the male' proved to be so accurate).

The AGM's format is pretty standard. The meeting will be opened by the President. The Secretary will read out the names of those apologising for their absence, trying not to snort in derision or laugh out loud. The minutes of the previous year's AGM will be unanimously accepted as a true record since many of those present can't even remember what they had for breakfast, let alone what was said at a meeting they slept through twelve months ago.

Now the Officers of the club present their reports. The President raises hopes of entertainment by opening with, *"I think my Presidential Year is best summarised in the immortal words of the actress to the bishop: 'Ooh, I enjoyed that more than I thought I would.'"* It's a false dawn. By the time we get to the end of the reports, the snores are audible.

We get on to agenda item, 'Resolutions'. The committee has proposed a couple of amendments to the club's Rules and Regulations. These are nodded through, both members and committee knowing that the amended rules will be as assiduously ignored as the unamended version.

Then it happens. The Treasurer stands, hoping upon hope to take advantage of the general stupor. Not a chance. The moment the trigger phrase, "next year's annual subscriptions" is uttered, the room comes alive. Backs straighten. Attentions are focussed. Penetrating questions are asked. Eventually a vote is taken, with the raised hands counted so as to be doubly sure, and the proposed subscription increases (never decreases) are grudgingly voted onto the statute book.

The timing is fortuitous. Wits have been sharpened by the economic debate, and just as well for it's the next item on the agenda that old hands know is the most dangerous. "Election of Officers," announces the President.

The practised ear can just make out the sound of butts on manoeuvres as those in the back row slide lower in their seats.

"I'm delighted to say that we have nominations for *almost* every position."

Our new bowler, ears not yet attuned to subtleties of AGM-speak, fails to spot the emphasis on the word 'almost' and continues to look interested.

"Only the position of Membership Secretary needs a nominee."

A solemn gaze sweeps around the room, which – from the President's point of view – now appears to have a completely empty back row. This gaze drifts past our new bowler like a searchlight, switches back ... and halts.

"Would anybody care to volunteer? One of our newer members perhaps?"

Arguments spring to the newbies' mind. *No time. No experience.* No hope. The President has seen all this before, from both sides of the fence.

"The current Membership Secretary will be only too pleased to hold their hand as they get their feet under the table."

Dumbly, our new bowler can't even raise an argument against the horribly mixed metaphor. A gulp. A nod. And they hear themselves saying, "I'll do it."

The effect is instantaneous. With an audible sigh of relief the back row suddenly reappears. A completely redundant voted is called for. Somehow, a forest of hands manages to shoot upwards and applaud at the same time.

To our newly-elected administrator, the remains of the meeting pass in a blur. As s/he drives home, a box of detritus from the delighted outgoing Membership Secretary on the passenger seat, little does s/he realise the problem ahead.

Not in joining the administrative side of the club; it's always an eye-opener to discover just how much effort is involved in running a bowls club. Not in doing the job, either; recruiting new members and watching them progress from beginners to seasoned players can be enormously satisfying.

No. The problem that every club officer has is that of getting rid of the job before they play their final end ...

Sometimes a little bit of encouragement from a few fellow bowlers is all that's needed to find a willing volunteer.

The Final End

Four new bowlers join their club on the same day. Let us anticipate things and call them Lead, Two, Three and Skip. They pass through the coaching sessions together and decide to form a Four. They play together thereafter – with a spectacular lack of success – until, conveniently for this story, they all expire on the same day. And so, just as they had in the beginning, they find themselves together once more – this time with St Peter at the Pearly Gates.

"Before you're allowed into heaven," St Peter tells them, "somebody has put in a good word for you." He turns to Skip. "So, tell me about Lead."

"Usually hopeless," growls Skip. "Either she left the first one short or stuck it miles behind. Then over-compensated and did the opposite."

St Peter nodded approvingly. "Lead tried to learn from her mistakes. Excellent. You're in, Lead." He turned back to Skip. "How about Two?"

Skip sighed. "No better. Usually found his line blocked by Lead's short ones so did his best to promote her bowls and make her look better than she was."

"Put another before himself," said St Peter, adding a second big tick to his ledger, "Well done Two, you're in." Once again, he turned back to Skip. "Three?"

"Totally bloody infuriating!" snapped Skip. "A good player but she never took things seriously enough. We go five down and what does she say? 'Never mind, the sun will still come up tomorrow.' Worst of all: 'It's only a game'!".

Skip took a deep breath in case his blood pressure was rising, then remembered that his blood no longer had a pressure. This was just as well, because St Peter had added a further tick to his ledger.

"Three kept matters in proportion," he smiled. "You're in, too."

As the Pearly Gates began to swing open Lead, Two and Three edged towards them.

"Hold on a minute," called St Peter. "Before you go in, how about Skip? What can you say in his favour?"

"Er ..." erred Lead.

"Ah ..." ahhed Two.

"Um ..." ummed Three.

"That's what I thought," said St Peter. *He snapped his ledger shut and pointed.* "The stairs down to the basement are that way, Skip."

The final end. It will come to us all. It may arrive quickly, like a 0-21 thrashing. It may arrive slowly, more akin to a multi-ended 20-21 game of attrition. But come it will.

Bill Shankly, legendary manager of Liverpool FC, once famously said,

> *"Football isn't a matter of life and death. It's much more important than that."*

That such complete tosh should have achieved the status of holy writ in the game is yet more evidence that when it comes to members of the football profession it's often a toss-up as to which is the greater, their IQ or their boot size.

Bowlers are much more realistic about the subject of death, and bowls clubs are no strangers to having their members pass away. The game may well be playable by ninety-five-year-olds, but every ninety-four-year-old is under no illusions about the odds of being around a year later to appreciate the fact.

The author's indoor club has an Obituaries Board located uncomfortably close to the steward's desk. He's

> **No entry into heaven, Mr Shankly, until you've done the lines you were set to write in purgatory:**
> **"At the end of the day, obviously, y'know like, I was bang out of order."**
> **Twenty billion times, if you please.**

well aware that one day he'll look across and find his own name there. [66]

The eulogy at a deceased bowler's funeral is always an illuminating experience. You will invariably discover that they had an interesting life before they took up the game. Astonishingly, you will regularly find yourself listening and wondering when bowls will even get a mention before slowly realising that, for them, the game

---

[66] Hopefully before using his club cash card to pay his rink fee. The prospect of spending aeons in purgatory as the steward works out how to process a refund is not a happy one.

was just a little bit of fancy embroidery – albeit valued - in the tapestry of their life. And, of course, there will be those for whom bowls was slap-bang in the centre, a huge source of enjoyment and companionship which got them out of bed in the mornings.

Whilst the late President's generous bequest had been welcome, the conditions laid down in the old buffer's will were proving to be rather irksome.

Bowls clubs are haunted.

This is not to suggest that the shades of late members prowl the green in the dead of night looking for the jack they couldn't find in life. It's simply that memories will be found in all manner of places.

We've already mentioned the sad corner containing old bowler's bowls which potential members invariably discover on a 'come and try' day. But there may well be other, jollier, reminders.

Players who've been successful in external competitions will have their names immortalised on the club's honours boards. [67] For triumphs that were especially noteworthy there may even be garlanded photographs on the clubhouse walls.

Bowlers who've served the club in high office are also likely to be listed prominently – especially if they've been successful in screwing money out of some funding organisation to help enhance the club's real estate.

Those left behind – Scoffers or Shakers, even – may have provided tangible reminders of their bowler's links to the club. A bench, a shrub for the garden surrounds, a new trophy to replace the battered one that the old bowler never quite managed to win: all these are fond signs either of what the club meant to the bowler or what the bowler meant to the club – invariably, both.

All these, important as they are, take second place to individual memories: those that bowlers create every time they set foot on the green.

"Do you remember her lovely laugh? You could tell what rink she was on without looking ..."

"Only bloke I knew who could draw to a sixpence and still look as miserable as sin ..."

"The skip that everybody enjoyed playing for ..."

"The skip that nobody enjoyed playing for ..."

---

[67] Even the names of unsuccessful bowlers might be found tucked away in the bottom corner of an honours board if they've generously, and shrewdly, donated the thing.

It's one of the big questions, of course. Probably the biggest. Is there bowls after death? Do we, in some mysterious way, play on?

Unlike many of the other bewildering topics covered in this book, this question is comparatively simple to answer. The only possibilities are No and Yes.

NO

In that case, if this spell on the green is all we have, what's the point in frowning? Why waste time brooding about what's done and done with?

YES

Now we're really into the world of conjecture. What will the great Bowling Green in the Sky be like? What would justify being called a bowler's heaven?

At first glance, these are questions that don't seem to need much thinking about. It will never rain, of course. The heavenly greens will never be less than perfectly true, and a bowler's every shot will finish right on the jack. That will do for starters.

Except that ... bowls is a competitive game. Who will our heavenly opponents be? Fellow angels, who will also put every shot bang on the jack? Or a touring team from Down Below, its players condemned to a never-ending wailing and gnashing of teeth as their shots go everywhere except where they want?

That sounds like either an eternity of draws or an eternity of massive wins. Boring, to say the least. And wouldn't the same go for playing the perfect shot every time? OK for the first couple of thousand years or so, perhaps, but for ever?

Where would be the unalloyed joy of pulling a fantastic shot out of the bag and wondering how the hell

> "Do me a favour, Lord. Don't make me the guardian angel for a Frowner."

you did it? Gone, because it would be happening every time.

The same goes for struggling to improve or winning unexpectedly – no more, because you couldn't improve on heavenly perfection and would win every time.

Even the pleasure of playing on a balmy evening, with the sun slowly setting over the green, wouldn't be fully appreciated if you'd never had to turn out in conditions that left every crevice oozing.

All gone, every one; all of the charm, the bewildering unpredictability, of the game excised and replaced by perfection. Sorry, but that sounds like hell to me.

No, the more you think about it, bowls as we have it – right here, right now – can't really be improved upon. Old bowlers may well get the shock of their deaths when they turn up for their first game on the heavenly green to discover that nothing's changed: that what we've had here all along has been heaven on earth.

And if that thought doesn't turn you into a Smiler, nothing will.

In Memoriam

Ann Antill
Viv Bramble
Maurice Brown
Edie Camilleri
Wally Chase
Laurie Clark
George Cole
John Coleman
Toni Donovan
Helen Francis
Tony Gambrill
Margaret Greenslade
Ron Greenslade
Alan Hagger
Cliff Hearsey
Richard Horler
Dave Hurst
Geoff Leech
Charlie Livingston
Janet Livingston
Mac Lowcock
Brian Maby
Malcolm McVicar
Derek Morgan
Doug Quade
Mal Rogers
Harry Savage
Ken Thorpe
John Travers
Mike Turner
Don Wares
June Westmore
Jim Wheeler

**And the answer was:
"Because they'd be mad not to!"**

Printed in Great Britain
by Amazon